This book belongs to

_____

...a woman after God's own heart.

Growing in Wisdom & Faith

Elizabeth George

HARVEST HOUSE PUBLISHERS
Eugene, Oregon 97402

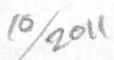

Cover by Terry Dugan Design, Minneapolis, Minnesota

Acknowledgments

As always, thank you to my dear husband, Jim George, M.Div., Th.M., for your able assistance, guidance, suggestions, and loving encouragement on this project.

GROWING IN WISDOM & FAITH
Copyright © 2001 Elizabeth George
Published by Harvest House Publishers
Eugene, Oregon 97402

ISBN 0-7369-0490-5

Printed in the United States of America

01 02 03 04 05 06 07 / BP-BG / 10 9 8 7 6 5 4 3 2

Contents

Foreword

For some time I have been looking for Bible studies that I could use each day that would increase my knowledge of God's Word. In my search, I found myself struggling between two extremes: Bible studies that required little time but also had little substance, or studies that were in-depth and demanded more time than I could give. I discovered that I wasn't alone—there were many other women like me who were busy yet desired to spend quality time studying God's Word.

That's why I became excited when Elizabeth George shared her desire to create a series of women's Bible studies that offered in-depth lessons that could be completed in just 15–20 minutes per day. When she completed the first study—on Philippians—I was eager to try it out. I had already studied Philippians many times, but this was the first time I had come to understand exactly how the whole book fit together and how it can truly be lived out in my life. Each lesson was simple but insightful—and was written especially to apply to me as a woman!

In the Woman After God's Own Heart™ Bible study series, Elizabeth takes you step by step through the Scriptures, sharing wisdom she has gleaned from more than 20 years as a women's Bible teacher. The lessons are rich and meaningful because they're rooted in God's Word and have been lived out in Elizabeth's life. Her thoughtful and personable guidance makes you feel as though you are studying right alongside her—as if she is personally mentoring you in the greatest aspiration you could ever pursue: to become a woman after God's own heart.

If you're looking for Bible studies that can help you grow stronger in your knowledge of God's Word even in the most demanding of schedules, I know you'll find this series to be a welcome companion in your daily walk with God.

—LaRae Weikert
Editorial Managing Director,
Harvest House Publishers

Before You Begin

In my book *A Woman After God's Own Heart,* I describe such a woman as one who ensures that God is first in her heart and the Ultimate Priority of her life. Then I share that one crucial way this desire can become reality is by nurturing a heart that abides in God's Word. To do so means that you and I must develop a root system anchored deep in God's Word.

Before you launch into this Bible study, take a moment to think about these aspects of a root system produced by the regular, faithful study of God's Word:

- *Roots are unseen*—You'll want to set aside time in solitude— "underground" if you will—to immerse yourself in God's Word and grow in Him.

- *Roots are for taking in*—Alone and with your Bible in hand, you'll want to take in and feed upon the truths of the Word of God and ensure your spiritual growth.

- *Roots are for storage*—As you form the habit of looking into God's Word, you'll find a vast, deep reservoir of divine hope and strength forming for the rough times.

- *Roots are for support*—Do you want to stand strong in the Lord? To stand firm against the pressures of life? The routine care of your roots through exposure to God's Word will cultivate you into a remarkable woman of endurance.[1]

I'm glad you've chosen this study out of my Woman After God's Own Heart™ Bible study series. My prayer for you is that the truths you find in God's Word through this study will further transform your life into the image of His dear Son and empower you to be the woman you seek to be: a woman after God's own heart.

In His love,

Elizabeth George

Lesson 1

Hearing the Heart of a Servant

James 1:1

First words tell us so much, quickly identifying who a person is and revealing their heart.

Well, dear one, today we meet James, the powerful leader of the early Christian church (see Acts 15). We read the first words he penned to Christians he had probably never met—and never would. There are only 20 words in this verse, but they are packed with meaning and information. Through this one short God-inspired utterance, we learn something about James and about the people to whom he wrote.

A few facts will help us as we work our way through this New Testament epistle. For instance, this letter was written

by James, to Jewish Christians in the first century,
from Jerusalem, about A.D. 48,
regarding putting faith to work in trials and hardship.

Now, let's learn about the man James and his message.

James 1:1

¹ James, a servant of God and of the Lord Jesus
Christ, to the twelve tribes which are scattered
abroad: Greetings.

God's Message...

1. *James.* The best way to learn more about James is to look
   at the few times he's mentioned in the Bible. Take a
   minute to jot down the information you can gather from
   these scriptures.

   Matthew 13:53-55—

   Acts 1:10-13 and 15:12-13—

   1 Corinthians 15:3-7—

   Galatians 1:18-19 and 2:7-9—

   Now, in a sentence or two, describe James.

2. *A servant.* James calls himself a servant. As a servant or
   bond-servant (or a *doulos* in the Greek language), James
   is stating outright that he considers himself to be a slave,
   one who is totally under the control of his master. In the
   words of another,

> _The Greek word *doulos* (slave, servant) refers to a position of complete obedience, utter humility, and unshakable loyalty. Obedience was the work, humility was the position, and loyalty was the relationship that a master expected from a slave.... There can be no greater tribute to a believer than to be known as God's obedient, humble, and loyal servant.[2]

Now note how several other writers of the New Testament epistles refer to themselves:

Romans 1:1—   2 Peter 1:1—

Philippians 1:1—   Jude 1—

Titus 1:1—   Revelation 1:1—

3. *A servant of God and of the Lord Jesus Christ.* Rather than name-dropping or boasting about the fact that he is related to Jesus, James chooses instead to refer to himself as a servant of *God* and of the *Lord Jesus Christ.* In James's thinking, these two names are equal because Jesus is God. Instead of referring to Jesus as his kin, James respectfully uses Jesus' full title:

> *Lord*—emphasizing His right to rule,

> *Jesus*—emphasizing His humanity, and

> *Christ*—emphasizing His Messiahship.

Note a few other titles and relationships we enjoy in the Lord Jesus Christ:

Matthew 12:46-50—   Ephesians 1:22—

John 10:11—   1 Timothy 2:5—

John 15:14-15—

4. *To the twelve tribes which are scattered abroad.* Exactly who were the twelve tribes? This phrase was used in James's day to indicate the entire Jewish nation. In this case, James uses "the twelve tribes" to refer to and to include all Jewish Christians outside Palestine.

   And how had these people come to be scattered? Earlier deportations accounted for the dispersion of some. Also, many Jews had moved to other lands in search of wealth and opportunity. So, by force and by choice, Jews were living throughout the Roman Empire.

   It's to these unknown fellow Jewish believers that James writes *Greetings*—a word that conveys a sense of joy and happiness and means "rejoice," or "be glad." James as much as states, "I wish you joy!"

...and Your Heart's Response

- James begins this powerful letter very simply...with only his name and an I.D. tag of "a servant of God and of the Lord Jesus Christ." Nothing flowery is said, no words of explanation are given, and nothing impressive is mentioned. How do you normally introduce yourself? Or, put another way, do you speak to impress...or to express? Or, put still another way, where is your heart and mind when you talk about yourself? Take a minute to honestly answer.

- How does James's reference to himself as a slave to God and to Christ challenge you? And when you consider that a slave was one whose will was not his own but who rather was committed to another, can you make such a claim?

- Read again these words describing a *doulos*—"A position of complete obedience, utter humility, and unshakable loyalty. Obedience was the work, humility was the position, and loyalty was the relationship that a master expected from a slave."

  Do you consider yourself to be God's obedient, humble, and loyal slave? If not, what's standing in the way of such a commitment…and what do you plan to do about it?

- A slave was obligated to perform his master's will completely, without question, and without delay. Are there any areas of disobedience in your life that make these actions of a slave an impossibility for you? If so, write out a plan of action here and now that will move you into a Master/slave relationship with Jesus Christ.

- Don't fail to spend time praying for whole-hearted obedience to God, His Word, and His will.

From the Heart of a Woman

Well, our first lesson is finished! As I'm sitting and thinking and praying about James, I'm struck by his powerful and straight-to-the-heart message. A servant. A slave. A *doulos*. How foreign in our self-oriented world! Yet James shows us the way to true greatness. Like James and like his half-brother Jesus, we are to take upon ourselves the form of a servant, humble ourselves, and become obedient to God (Philippians 2:7-8). What does that mean, to you and to me, as women who yearn to follow after God's own heart?

> *It means obedience.* As slaves we're to know no law but our master's word; to have no rights of our own; to be the absolute possession of our master; and to give our master unquestioning obedience.

> *It means humility.* "Slave" defines a woman who thinks not of privileges but of duties, not of rights but of obligations. It's the word for one whose self is lost in the service of God.

> *It means loyalty.* "Slave" describes the woman who lives out her faith by doing all for God. Personal profit and personal preference do not enter into her calculations; her loyalty is to Him.

> *It means joining the ranks of "the great ones."* "Slave" was the title by which "the great ones" of the Old Testament were known—Moses, Joshua, Caleb, the patriarchs Abraham, Isaac, and Jacob, Job, Isaiah, and the prophets. By choosing to take the title *doulos,* we set ourselves in the great succession of those who found their freedom and their peace and their glory in perfect submission to the will of God. The only greatness to which we Christians can ever aspire is that of being the slave of God.[3]

Now, dear woman after God's own heart, can you fill in the blank with your name, "_____, a servant of God and of the Lord Jesus Christ"? May we learn to prize this title above all others in the world! May we willfully take upon ourselves the title and conduct of "slave" and join the ranks of those like James who were honored not only for who they were, but for whom they served—the living God!

Lesson 2

Living in Faith

We've started! We're off on our study of the epistle of James, a New Testament book about living in genuine faith. I know we covered many important points in our first lesson about James, both the man and his epistle. But we did omit one vital fact for our understanding—*why* James wrote this letter. There are two main reasons for this little letter.

External Problems—First of all, those to whom James wrote were experiencing a number of external problems and trials. His readers (as we'll see later in our study) were being persecuted by their own non-believing Jewish countrymen and oppressed by the rich and powerful. They also suffered physical afflictions from various sources. Plus they were foreigners who had fled from their own country—truly strangers in a strange land.

Internal Problems—In addition to problems from without, there were also problems from within. When you look at this list you'll more than likely recognize yourself and some of your own challenges. (And you'll also recognize why the book of James is so practical to you and me today!)

- Spiritual distress
- Wrong doctrine caused by wrong living
- Wrong attitudes toward the goodness of God and His gifts
- A general low spiritual state

These led to

- Indulgence in unbridled speech
- Growth of strife and factions among themselves
- The adoption of a worldly spirit

And so, dear one, James wrote to counteract these wrong thoughts and actions. He set about to explain the nature of genuine faith. And he exhorted his fellow Christians (including us!) to live out their faith in practical day-to-day ways. He addressed their *duties* as Christians and challenged them to *live* the Christian life, not just to profess it. In other words, they were to "walk their talk."

You'll find in the book of James inspiring encouragement to live in a godly manner, to live up to your faith. However, you'll also find warnings about slipping back into old un-Christian ways of living. James's clarion call to us is to live a productive faith, to live out our faith by deeds of faith. So be ready with an open heart, my friend.

I feel I must warn you to be prepared, as we go through James's epistle, for his writing style. James is blunt! He never beats around the bush about any topic, no matter how delicate. And he also gets right to the point...as we witness right now and right here in verse 2.

James 1:2-4

² My brethren, count it all joy when you fall into various trials,

³ knowing that the testing of your faith produces patience.

⁴ But let patience have its perfect work, that you may be perfect and complete, lacking nothing.

God's Message...

1. What initial admonition does James give (verse 2)?

And what word does he use to describe the trials they will encounter (verse 2)?

2. James presents a sort of "bad news/good news" scenario here. Verse 2 contained the bad news, the fact that those he is writing to would most definitely experience trials. In fact, many and varied trials! But now James comes along behind the bad news with the good news. According to verse 3, what is the good news?

3. When patience or endurance has finished its work, what changes will have taken place in the readers' lives (verse 4)?

a.   b.   c.

(Just a note here: This is not sinless perfection, but a right relationship with God that is lived out in obedience.)

4. According to James, why can we count on all trials to become an occasion for rejoicing (verses 3-4)?

...and Your Heart's Response

- Oh, my! I was just recently looking for a greeting card for a friend who is suffering and needed a word of encouragement. I had my choice of any number of cards that advised my friend to...

> Withdraw (from the problem...or problem person)
> Win (in whatever the issue was)
> Give in (and have a good cry)
> Compromise (for the sake of peace)

And yet what does our dear, blunt-but-wise James advise (verse 2)?

- Can you list some ways Christians (and you, too!) mistakenly view trials?

- How do you normally regard the trials you encounter? Or, if those who know you best were asked this question, what would they report?

- Consider the following progression from verses 3-4:

> TRIALS work to
> TEST MY FAITH which
> PRODUCES PATIENCE which makes me
> PERFECT AND COMPLETE, LACKING NOTHING.

Jot down the most pressing trial you are facing (or "falling into") right now. Then comment on what new light these truths about trials shed on your problem.

- What will you do to adjust your attitude toward trials so that it matches up with what James says here about trials and testing?

- Finally, how do these truths encourage or rebuke you?

From the Heart of a Woman

How can something be so sobering and so exciting at the same time? That's what I'm wondering about these three powerful verses! My heart is sobered…by the fact that trials will most certainly come my way. It's a given of the Christian life. James said *when* you fall into various trials, not *if* you fall into them. And my heart is inspired…at the thought of becoming a woman of even greater faith.

Before we put away this lesson, I'm thinking about two "Yes, but how?" questions: *How* can we count our trials as joy? And *how* can we ensure that our faith grows in—and in spite of—our trials? Take to heart these two answers.

First, *by the use of your mind.* Remember that counting trials as joy has to do with the mind, not the emotions. Your emotions cannot do this, but your mind must. No matter what your emotions "feel" (devastated, discouraged, etc.) and no matter what your body feels (pain, exhaustion, etc.), we're to do what the Nike shoe and clothing ads tell us— "Just do it!" Just count it all joy! Please, don't wonder. Don't worry. Don't question. Don't guess. Don't fret. Don't rebel.

And especially, don't balk! Just count your trials as joy—knowing that you will eventually begin reaping the blessings of joy, patience, perfection, and completion. The joyous outcome of your trials will be greater Christian maturity and greater faith.

Which brings us to the second "how," *by the use of your faith.* You and I must look at each trial with the eye of faith. Why? Because the eye of faith will *see* the hand of God in all of life. And only faith can do God's kind of bookkeeping and place each trial in the joy column. You see, dear one, when you suffer you must *believe* in the goodness of God and in His perfecting process of you and your faith. You must *believe* that He and He alone knows what He is doing. You must *believe* during the painful times that God loves you and is in perfect control of all things. You must *believe* in the greater-yet-veiled purposes of God. And you must *believe* in the results of your testings.

So be encouraged and forge ahead through your troubles! As the Bible reminds us, "...we do not look at the things which are seen, but at the things which are not seen. For the things which are seen are temporary, but the things which are not seen are eternal" (2 Corinthians 4:18). Now *that's* the way the eye of faith looks at trials!

I sure do hope that this list of "Withouts" persuades you to press on in your quest to grow in wisdom and faith.

A List of "Withouts"

Without trials there can be no maturity.

Without clouds there can be no silver lining.

Without clouds there can be no appreciation of sunshine.

Without rain there can be no rainbow.

Without rain there can be no vegetation.

Without the stress of the storm we cannot realize the worth of an anchor.

Without darkness there can be no rest.

Without darkness we cannot see the stars.

Without night there can be no sunrise.

Without threshing we cannot use the wheat.

Without injury and irritation the oyster will not produce a pearl.

Without a hammer and chisel the stone cannot become a statue, a work of art, a masterpiece.

Without crushing the flowers there can be no perfume.

Without trials we cannot be like Jesus.

Lesson 3

Discovering the Secret to Wisdom

James 1:5-8

There are two kinds of secrets in this world—those that are worth keeping and those that are too good to keep! Well, my friend, James has a secret that is definitely too good to keep, and that's the secret to wisdom in dealing with our trials. We might well imagine James declaring, "Let me tell you a secret—a secret that will revolutionize your life as you encounter the various trials life sends your way! A secret that will bring about greater endurance, greater character, greater wisdom, and greater faith!"

As we dream about possessing these desirable qualities and wonder how we might grasp them, James tells us the secret in one word—*ask* for it! Pay close attention as James elaborates on this simplistic advice and leads us in a step-by-step plan for attaining the wisdom for handling our trials! He writes...

James 1:5-8

⁵ If any of you lacks wisdom, let him ask of God, who gives to all liberally and without reproach, and it will be given to him.

⁶ But let him ask in faith, with no doubting, for he who doubts is like a wave of the sea driven and tossed by the wind.

⁷ For let not that man suppose that he will receive anything from the Lord;

⁸ he is a double-minded man, unstable in all his ways.

God's Message...

1. **Step One** for wisdom is to **Ask**—How does James begin his instructions in verse 5? If...

And what does he advise (verse 5)?

What do these proverbs say about asking for wisdom?

> Proverbs 1:5—

> Proverbs 3:13-15—

> Proverbs 4:7—

We know that James was the half-brother of Jesus. What did Jesus say about asking (Matthew 7:7-8)?

2. **Step Two** for wisdom is to **Ask God**—James says that *if* you lack wisdom for handling difficulties, *then* you are to ask God for it. How does James describe God (verse 5)?

   a.   b.

   And what is the promise given to those who ask God for wisdom (verse 5)?

3. **Step Three** for wisdom is to **Ask God in faith**—what caution does James give for asking for wisdom in verse 6?

   How does James illustrate his point from nature (verse 6)?

   What is the danger in doubting (verse 7)?

   Further describe the one who doubts (verse 8).

...and Your Heart's Response

As we think about James's secret to growing in wisdom (asking God in faith) and about growing in faith, let's not miss his message regarding faith. James says...

- *Think about the act of asking.* Where do you normally turn first when you need wisdom, when you need help, when you need advice? Do you get on the phone, or do you get on your knees? What can you do to "remember" to boldly ask God for His wisdom (Hebrews 4:16) the next time you are in trouble?

  (As someone has remarked, "When life knocks you to your knees, you're in the proper position to pray!")

- *Think about the Person of God.* Note again here what God does when we ask Him for wisdom (verse 5)…

…and what God does *not* do when we ask Him for wisdom (verse 5).

How does the fact of God's "liberal" giving and refusal to "reproach" encourage you to approach Him?

- *Think about asking in faith.* How you ask God for wisdom is as important as asking Him for it. You can ask in faith or you can ask with doubts. Hear these insights from Moody Bible Institute's Dr. Harold D. Foos regarding the dilemma of the doubting man…or woman.

*T*he doubter is like a wind-tossed wave, driven hither and yon, up and down, back and forth, at the whim of the wind. Like a rudderless ship, such a man has no direction and no control. Do you know anyone like that? This way today, that way tomorrow; up yesterday, down today; at the mercy of varying circumstances because he has not anchored his life in the Word of God and has not sought direction by the Spirit of God.

*G*od does not answer such a person. This fact does not stem from a flaw in the character of God or in a lack of desire on God's part…but is the result of a failing in the one who asks.[4]

Beloved, James is calling you (and me) to get into the
race of faith. He is calling you to be sure your mind is
made up about what you want. Do you truly want
wisdom for handling your problems? Then you must go
to the only true source—to the "giving" God who
bestows wisdom for managing life's trials. And you must
go to Him wholeheartedly, trusting in full faith, doubting
nothing.

Evaluate whether or not you are growing as a woman of
faith, a woman who asks God wholeheartedly, trusts Him
completely, and doubts nothing.

	Yes	No
Are you completely convinced that God's way is always best?	____	____
Do you treat God's Word like mere human advice, something you can take or discard?	____	____
Do you vacillate between your feelings, the world's advice, and God's commands?	____	____
Do you believe that God cares about you, that He is powerful, and that He is good?	____	____

These are serious questions. Be aware that your answers
may call for serious prayer and serious changes!

From the Heart of a Woman

How many times a day do you need God's wisdom, my
friend? As I write these words, it's almost twelve noon, and

I've already needed God's wisdom for a variety of issues (trials)—common and uncommon.

> Should I have my devotions first on this very busy day after a three-day holiday weekend, or should I get things rolling and have them later?

> What three messages will I share at an upcoming event? (They need the titles...NOW!)

> Should I get into fine-tuning our tax preparations this morning (in lieu of writing) or wait until this evening?

> What should I eat today to maintain high energy for writing and yet watch out for extra pounds?

Other women I know faced difficult situations today ranging from...

> What should I do about my one-year-old who strikes out at my face in anger? to...

> What should I do about my husband's infatuation with a younger single woman?

We all need wisdom for dealing with our trials—God's good wisdom. And we can thank Him that all we need to do is ask Him for it with a heart full of faith...and it will be given! So the next time you face your own trials or dilemmas, instead of praying for the removal of your test, ask God for His wisdom to handle it His way. Just stop, look, and listen before you proceed ahead.

> **Stop** before you do anything. This gives you time to consult the Lord before you act.

Look to the Lord. Boldly ask, "Lord, what do you want me to do here? How do you want me to respond? What's the right thing to do? I want to do things *Your* way."

Listen for His wisdom. A heart of faith believes God hears our cry for help...*and* answers (1 Peter 3:12; Psalm 116:1-2; 138:3).

Proceed. A heart of faith also believes God's wisdom is best and responds in obedience, without doubt.

These actions and attitudes of faith, dear one, make up the secret to wisdom. We *will* face trial after trial, but we now know the secret of *how* to face them. Now, let's remember to put the secret to use and further grow in wisdom and in our faith!

Benefiting Through Trials

James 1:9-12

Whenever I think about the reality of trials and the fact that they produce patience and maturity, it helps me to think of a boat. My thoughts run this way: Each trial that comes my way is like a body of water that must be crossed. And there's only one way to cross a body of water, and that's to get into a boat, push away from the comfort of the shore—from the known, from my present state of spiritual growth—and set sail. To successfully navigate and "pass" each new trial, I must sail from Point A to Point B. I must get into the boat, I must set sail from Point A, and then I must *stay* in the boat until it reaches the other side, Point B. There are no shortcuts!

The act of sailing is quite demanding! I know—I've done it! And so is the act of enduring each trial until it's over. And for me to endure means that I can't "jump ship." I can't bail out. I can't panic. I can't waver in my commitment to ride it out. No, I must *stay* in the boat. I can't give in to fear or dread. I can't throw in the towel when I think I've had enough. I can't change my mind. I can't falter at danger or doubt. I must simply hang on for dear life and *stay* in the boat!

Yes, enduring trials is difficult. Each new test challenges me to use the strength and wisdom and maturity I already possess. And it challenges my previously hard-won faith as I must once again trust the Lord to enable me. But the really good news is that when I reach the other side of each trial, when my boat strikes shore at Point B, growth has occurred! Wonderful, noticeable, real spiritual growth!

It's the same for you, too, dear one. Increased wisdom, faith, and spiritual maturity await you on the other side of each and every trial that is successfully endured, regardless of your position in life, as you trust God! Trials benefit every one of us, and that's James's good news for us in this next passage. Read on!

James 1:9-12

⁹ Let the lowly brother glory in his exaltation,

¹⁰ but the rich in his humiliation, because as a flower of the field he will pass away.

¹¹ For no sooner has the sun risen with a burning heat than it withers the grass; its flower falls and its beautiful appearance perishes. So the rich man also will fade away in his pursuits.

¹² Blessed is the man who endures temptation; for when he has been proved, he will receive the crown of life which the Lord has promised to those who love Him.

God's Message...

Right away in these few verses we notice two kinds of people in two different sets of circumstances, each presenting its own kind of trial and each resulting in the perfection and purification of faith.

The Lowly

To be lowly means to be of low means, of low degree, or of low position. What does James say this brother's response to his position in life is to be (verse 9)?

According to verse 12, what will the proper, godly handling of his lowly estate reap?

And what will it indicate (verse 12)?

However, to receive the blessings, what must he first do (verse 12)?

The Rich

What is the rich man to glory in (verse 10)?

What illustration from nature does James use to show how quickly a man's riches—or the man himself—may pass away (verses 10-11)? Describe the process.

What will the proper, godly handling of his wealth reap for this man (verse 12)?

And what will it prove (verse 12)?

However, to receive the blessings, what must he first do (verse 12)?

...and Your Heart's Response

Too often the lowly are looked down upon and the wealthy are looked up to. But James gives an assignment to each. Look again at both and apply God's message to your personal situation. And don't forget to study the opposite set of circumstances so you'll know how to properly view, appreciate, understand, encourage, and pray for others.

The Lowly

Suppose you are in poverty, the brother (or, in our case, the "sister") in humble circumstances. You're called upon by James to rejoice and to glory in the fact that as a Christian you're elevated. Do you wonder how this could be true?

- Look at 1 Peter 1:3-6 and then count and list your blessings as a Christian—no matter how poor or insignificant you seem to be.

- Add to these powerful truths the fact that we are "children of God" and "joint heirs with Christ" (Romans 8:16,17) and you can see why, even if we're of lowly estate, we can "glory" and "rejoice"! Are you rejoicing, dear one? How about writing out a prayer of thanksgiving for your "spiritual riches" in Christ Jesus?

The Rich

Suppose, on the other hand, that you fall into this category, that you are blessed with wealth and material goods. Well, James has a word for you, too! James says something to this effect: "Be sure you put no store in your riches! For life is uncertain. As quickly as the newly-risen sun wilts and withers the grass, so your riches can disappear. Don't place your trust in external things you can lose in a second! Trust instead (and rejoice) in the Lord and in the eternal riches only He can provide."

- What do you consider to be God's greatest gift(s) to you? Why?

- What blessings can you count on in Christ—even if you lose all that you have?

Just today I read this story in a devotional. I admit, I found it to be somewhat disheartening, but, as I'm writing about "losing all," it immediately came to mind. I share it here because it demonstrates the Who of our vast wealth and the seat of our Hope as believers.

> The story is told of a godly woman who, having buried one of her children, sat alone in her sadness, yet had ease of heart when she read *The Lord liveth* [Psalm 18:46]. Then another child died, still she remained calm and trustful as she said, "Comforts die, but God lives." Then the heaviest blow of all fell upon her, for her beloved husband died, and she became almost overwhelmed with sorrow. But her surviving child, having observed what

before she spoke to comfort herself, said to her disconsolate mother, "Is God dead, Mother? Is God dead?" This reached the sorrowing woman's heart, and her former confidence in a *living* God returned.[5]

It's true, dear one. Whether we lose our wealth, our health, or our loved ones, God is alive forevermore, and His promises to take care of us in any and every circumstance abide forever. As James shows us, we can "glory" in our humiliation, in our losses, because when all our "riches" are gone, we will still belong to the God of the universe. We'll still be His beloved child, blessed with every spiritual blessing in heavenly places in Christ (Ephesians 1:3)!

Benefiting Through Trials...

...That's the name of this lesson. As you weigh the blessings and benefits you enjoy when you endure the trials that come your way, can you now see why you must "stay in the boat" when trials test you? Dear woman of faith, you receive a four-fold promise that when your boat touches the shore at Point B: 1) You will be blessed. 2) You will have proved and further grown in your faith. 3) You are assured a "crown," a symbol of God's approval. 4) You will have proved your love for the Lord.

- How do these truths about testing change your view of your trials?

- And what will you do to "glory" in your next trial? How will verse 12 encourage you?

From the Heart of a Woman

I can't believe that so much sobering truth can be covered in so few verses! The poor, the rich, and everyone in between! We've looked at them all. And in the end we know one thing—the ground at the foot of the cross is level. No person stands higher than another. Trials are the great equalizer, leveling all believers to dependence on God. Therefore we persevere…knowing that we will receive the blessing of the crown of life which the Lord has promised to those who love Him (…and we do!).

I can find no better way to end our lesson than to share this priceless bit of wisdom from an unknown saint!

Paradoxes of Prayer

I asked God for strength, that I might achieve.
I was made weak, that I might learn humbly to
   obey…
      I asked for health, that I might do greater things.
      I was given infirmity, that I might do better
         things…
I asked for riches, that I might be happy.
I was given poverty that I might be wise…
      I asked for power, that I might have the praise
         of men.
      I was given weakness, that I might feel the need
         of God…
I asked for all things, that I might enjoy life.
I was given life, that I might enjoy all things…
      I got nothing that I asked for—
      but everything I had hoped for.
Almost despite myself, my unspoken prayers were
   answered—
I am among all, most richly blessed![6]

Lesson 5

Understanding Temptation
James 1:13-16

As we approach yet another bit of wisdom from James on "The Three Ts"—trials, testing, and temptation—let this story about developing a healthy root system lead you to stand strong in the Lord, so that you may grow strong in your faith. It's about...

> ...the process used in bygone days for growing the trees that became the main masts for military and merchant ships. The great shipbuilders first selected a tree located on the top of a high hill as a potential mast. Then they cut away all of the surrounding trees that would shield the chosen one from the force of the wind. As the years went by and the winds blew fiercely against the tree, the tree only grew stronger until finally it was strong enough to be the foremast of a ship.[7]

A woman of faith, dear one, has grown into such a one *because of* her trials, testings, and temptations. Amid the sternest of trials, she's been forced to either topple or lean...*or* to thrust her roots down even deeper toward "the Rock of Ages" so that she might triumph and stand firm, defying even the worst hurricanes of temptation!

Do you want a stronger faith? Do you desire to grow into a remarkable woman of endurance? Then let's pay close attention as James teaches us the importance of *Understanding Temptation*.

James 1:13-16

¹³ Let no one say when he is tempted, "I am tempted by God"; for God cannot be tempted by evil, nor does He Himself tempt anyone.

¹⁴ But each one is tempted when he is drawn away by his own desires and enticed.

¹⁵ Then, when desire has conceived, it gives birth to sin; and sin, when it is fully grown, brings forth death.

¹⁶ Do not be deceived, my beloved brethren.

God's Message...

Just to bring us up to date, we've already learned that God brings special challenges into the life of each believer so that his or her faith can grow. Well, today James teaches us two ways we can respond to trials, testing, and temptation. One of them is the "wrong" way and the other is the "right" way. Let's learn all we can about this important subject, the truth about temptation.

1. We already know that trials *will* come (verse 2). What does James say his readers are *not* to do when they're tested and tempted (verse 13)?

   And what two facts does James give to prove that this reaction is improper or wrong (verse 13)?

   a.

   b.

2. But James quickly shows us the source of temptation. According to verse 14, what is that source?

3. Fill in this chart showing the progression of temptation from verses 14 and 15: Each person is tempted

   When he is _____ and _____
   by _____.

   Then once desire is conceived, it leads to _____
   which when fully grown leads to _____.

   Simply charted, the progression would be
   _____ ➔ _____ ➔ _____

4. What warning does James then give (verse 16)?

...and Your Heart's Response

The "wrong" response to temptation.

- Let's think again about the "wrong" response to testing and temptation. In a word, who is most definitely *not* responsible for our temptations (verse 13)?

  And who *is* most definitely responsible for our temptations (verse 14)?

  And bringing the truth about temptation even closer to home, who is most definitely *not* responsible for *your* temptations...

  ...and who is most definitely responsible for *your* temptations?

- Take a look at Genesis 3:1-13. When God questioned Adam, what answer did Adam give (verse 12)?

  Where did he put the blame? (Be careful—there's a two-part answer here!)

  And when God questioned Eve, what answer did she give (verse 13)?

  Where did she put the blame?

- Now note Exodus 32:19-24. Who did Aaron blame for the golden calf (verses 22-24)?

Excusing and Accusing

*I*t's truly amazing how many excuses we can come up with when we give in to temptation instead of persevering and passing the test! And it's equally amazing how many people we can manage to blame in our excuse-making. Here's a sampler of excuses:

"It's the other person's fault."

"I couldn't help it."

"Everybody's doing it."

"It was just a mistake."

"Nobody's perfect."

"I didn't know it was wrong."

"The devil made me do it."

"I was pressured into it."[8]

*A*nd sometimes we even blame things! "The alarm clock didn't go off." "My car wouldn't start." "The dog ate my paper." Even Aaron said in essence, "It [the golden calf] just came out of the fire!"

The "right" response to temptation.

As we've noted before, James wrote his little letter to correct some big errors in his readers' behavior and in their thinking and theology. They clearly needed help with their understanding of God...and of the nature of sin. In these few logical, succinct, to-the-point verses, James sets everyone straight about the matter of sin and temptation. We've already seen the *wrong* response. Now we get to grapple with the *right* response to trials, testing, and temptation.

- If we're not to "blame" God, Satan, others, or our circumstances, then who does that leave to "blame"? And why (verse 14)?

- James warns us to this effect as we read: "Watch out for your own desires! Unchecked desires lead to sin...which leads to death!" It's clear to see that we must be aware of temptations *and* check them, nip them in the bud. Note one situation where temptation went unchecked.

Achan at Ai—When Achan appeared before Joshua, the leader of God's people, what explanation did he give to account for his sin (Joshua 7:21)?

  I _____ the spoils, the goods,

  I _____ them, and

  I _____ them. And then

  I _____ them.

Did you notice the initial temptation? And did you notice the progression of the temptation until it became full-blown, active, willful sin? How did this situation end for Achan (verse 25)?

- As you think about Achan and the progression of his sin and its awful consequences, write out three or four checkpoints or safeguards or boundaries you could set for yourself that would help you deal with temptation before it gives birth to sin. (Remember—temptation in itself is not sin. But *the failure to resist* temptation is.)

From the Heart of a Woman

I hope you have "gotten" the message James is sending our way. (And I hope, too, that you got the message from Question 3 and the simple-yet-awful progression of sin, that unchecked *desires* lead to *sin* which leads to *death*.) I also hope this little list will help you to grasp—and do something about—James's message regarding our understanding about temptation.

Be—not deceived! James warns us to stop being deceived about the nature of God and the real source of temptation and to grow up in our understanding and in our behavior.

Be—ware and be aware of blaming, of blaming God and others. Instead...

Be—ware and be aware of your own sin.

Be—ware and be aware of these sources of temptation— the world, the flesh, and the devil (1 John 2:15-16).

Be—ware and be aware of wishing to be deprived of trials. They are, as Charles Spurgeon, famed preacher-of-old, noted, "the necessary attendants of spiritual advancement."[9]

Lesson 6

Learning the Truth About God

James 1:17-18

"My beloved brethren" (verse 16). For James, the abrupt and brusque communicator of truth, these are indeed sweet words! I'm sure you agree with me that James's previous message was a hard one! His instruction about sin and temptation was shot straight at the heart of every believer. It was a warning. It was a correction. It was a reality check. And it was sobering!

But James is also a man of great wisdom. His letter is full of it! Indeed, the book of James is considered to be the New Testament book of proverbs, the ABCs of wisdom. And so this wise, loving, half-brother of the Lord softens the blow with these tender words, "my beloved brethren." He knows (and I hope you do, too!—we can learn a lesson in wisdom here from James!) that hard words and truths go down easier when we know the one delivering them truly loves us...and the Lord.

And so, "my beloved brethren," we will move on from the dark truth about sin and temptation to the brilliant truth about God. Read on...and revel in His goodness.

James 1:17-18

¹⁷ Every good gift and every perfect gift is from above, and comes down from the Father of lights, with whom there is no variation or shadow of turning.

¹⁸ Of His own will He brought us forth by the word of truth, that we might be a kind of firstfruits of His creatures.

God's Message

1. Let's take a look backward in James 1 to ground ourselves before we move on to this topic. Looking back at verses 2-4, what general topic is being addressed?

   And looking back at verses 13-16, what were these Christians erroneously thinking about God?

   And what warning did James give them in verse 16?

2. Now let's turn to the passage at hand, to verses 17-18. What are the two *everys* that James mentions here?

   a. Every _____   b. Every _____

And what does James say is the source of all goodness and all giving (verse 17)?

Exactly how does James describe the nature of God (verse 17)?

3. James uses an illustration from astronomy to describe the nature of "lights" (the sun, moon, and stars) in contrast with the nature of God (verse 17). Unlike the "lights"...

...James states that with God there is *no* _____ and *no* _____.

4. Next James mentions one *good* thing God had already done for the readers. What is it (verse 18)?

And what two forces accomplished this wonderful act (verse 18a)?

a.   b.

And what purpose or result does God desire (verse 18b)?

...and Your Heart's Response

- *The character of God.* Take a minute to jot down the teachings about the character of God that are mentioned in these two verses.

In light of these truths, what must you *never* think about God?

Conversely, what must you *always* think about God?

- *The goodness of God.* Indeed, goodness is one of God's attributes. And, as we learned in our previous lesson, God, because of His goodness, cannot tempt us with sin nor cause evil in our life. What did Jesus say about God and His goodness in Matthew 19:17?

And what did Jesus have to say about the gifts God gives in Matthew 7:11?

How does knowing about the goodness of God change (or should change!) the way you view the things in your life, the things God allows and disallows for you?

- *The immutability of God.* God also is unchanging, immutable. Nature and the lights (the sun, moon, and stars) bring us seasons, days, and years. Even the earth turns on its axis and rotates around the sun, casting moving shadows and changes of vision and angle. How does it comfort you to know that your God *never* changes, *never* varies, *never* wavers?

And how do you think this truth about God—the fact of His unchanging nature—can help you go through testing and endure temptation?

- *The salvation of your soul.* Surely the best "good gift" God gives to us is spiritual birth! And the Word of His truth is the gospel, the Good News of salvation through Jesus Christ. This Word is extended to us through reading God's Word, the Bible, and hearing His Word preached.

  Evaluate your own passion for the Bible. Are you reading it regularly? Are you putting yourself regularly under the teaching of faithful preachers and teachers of God's Word? And, speaking of salvation, are you sharing the truth about God from the Bible with others who need to be "born again" to the new birth? Lay out a plan of action to grow in each of these three areas:

  a.   Reading the Word

  b.   Hearing the Word

  c.   Sharing the Word

And just a note about the "firstfruits." We learned earlier that James is writing to Jewish believers. They would know full well what James was referring to—the Old Testament practice of offering the first of the crops to God as worship (see Exodus 34:22; Leviticus 23:9-10; Deuteronomy 26:9-11). Believers in Christ are a new creation in Him, examples—or firstfruits—of God's goodness and a living testimony of what Christ can do in a life. This might be a good time to:

  a.   Thank God again for His goodness in your salvation.

  b.   Evaluate your life as an example. Do you need to make any changes in order to better live up to your label as a firstfruit, as an offering to God?

From the Heart of a Woman

"The most important thing in the world is not to know the Lord's will but to know the Lord."[10] That's wise advice! And this passage from James has certainly shown us some of the glories of our Lord—His character, His goodness, His immutability, and His salvation. It's been a lot to take in!

I hope that these notes from a sermon entitled "The Father of the Lights" will shed some "devotional light" upon God's majestic attributes.

We worship, not light, but "the Father of the lights." Consider some of the lights of which God is the Father.

Sun-light. The sun is a great work of God. Our whole world gets all its light from the sun. Even moon-light and star-light are reflections of the light of the sun.

Truth-light. This gives us the light of knowledge. We have this truth-light in the Bible, "a lamp shining in a dark place," and in the Savior, "the Light of the world," the dear Son of "the Father of the lights."

Heaven-light. The home of God in heaven is full of light. In hell, all is darkness; on earth, there is mingled light and darkness; in heaven, there is only light. "There shall be no night there." God and the Lamb are "the light thereof." And everything in heaven reflects its light—the jasper walls, the pearly gates, the golden streets, the crystal river, the white robes. It is holiness that is the light of heaven. All there is pure. Grace-light, when a good man dies, blazes up into glory-light. And all the holiness of heaven streams from the Holy, Holy, Holy One—"the Father of the lights."[11]

Living in Obedience

James 1:19-27

I can still remember one of the very first "babysteps" I took as a new Christian just setting out on my quest for spiritual growth and a growing faith. Our church offered a series of evening classes, and I enrolled in the one listed as "Spiritual Boot Camp." It appealed to me and fit my desire for instruction—even hard instruction. I wanted to be shaped up, disciplined, and shown the basics. I needed to firm up my beliefs, to be told the do's and don'ts of being a Christian, to toughen up, and to make some serious changes.

Well, my friend, I think James's passage right here is a sort of "Spiritual Boot Camp." It's full of advice for growing, for changing our behavior, for beefing up and shaping up our faith. And what I like best is his list of do's and don'ts. He tells it like it is. He leaves nothing out. When he's done

49

with us, there's no guesswork or wondering. We know *exactly* what to do and what not to do.

Let's let the Master's sergeant do his thing. "Listen up!", we might well imagine him saying…

James 1:19-27

[19] Therefore, my beloved brethren, let every man be swift to hear, slow to speak, slow to wrath;

[20] for the wrath of man does not produce the righteousness of God.

[21] Therefore lay aside all filthiness and overflow of wickedness, and receive with meekness the implanted word, which is able to save your souls.

[22] But be doers of the word, and not hearers only, deceiving yourselves.

[23] For if anyone is a hearer of the word and not a doer, he is like a man observing his natural face in a mirror;

[24] for he observes himself, goes away, and immediately forgets what kind of man he was.

[25] But he who looks into the perfect law of liberty and continues in it, and is not a forgetful hearer but a doer of the work, this one will be blessed in what he does.

[26] If anyone among you thinks he is religious, and does not bridle his tongue but deceives his own heart, this one's religion is useless.

[27] Pure and undefiled religion before God and the Father is this: to visit orphans and widows in their trouble, and to keep oneself unspotted from the world.

God's Message...

1. Right off, James gives us three commands, three "do's" (verse 19). What are they?

   a.   b.   c.

   And why (verse 20)?

   What does James say will help us do this (verse 21)?

   Lay aside...

   Receive...

   And what will this accomplish (verse 21)?

2. Get ready for another important "do" and "don't." James says in verse 22:

   "Do" be...

   And "don't" be...

3. How does James describe the person who is "a hearer of the word and not a doer" (verses 23-24)?

   What does the person who is "blessed" do (verse 25)?

4. And finally, James addresses the evidences of true piety, of a true religion. What are they (verses 26-27)?

   Verse 26—

   Verse 27—(this one has two parts)

...and Your Heart's Response

These verses and James's message can be divided into three main points:

- *First, receive the Word*—Look again at the three commands in verse 19. "Every" woman (says James), must do battle to control her tongue. And it's a fact—if our mouth is open, our ears are usually shut! As the ancient philosopher Zeno of Cyprus has noted, "We have two ears but only one mouth, that we may hear more and speak less."[12] In order to receive the Word of God, James says we're to be...

  quick to hear and actively, carefully listening when it is being taught,

  slow to speak so that what we say is well thought out, edifies those who hear, accurately reflects the Scriptures, and honors the Lord,

  slow to anger when confronted by the Word of God or others disagree with our understanding of Scripture.

What is your normal pattern when it comes to hearing and speaking? Would you consider yourself to be on the quiet side or the talkative side. A hearer or a "yapper"? Ask God to help you identify your tendencies.

Then there's the matter of anger. The word used here for anger (*orgé*) refers to an inner, deep resentment that seethes and smolders, not to an explosive outburst of temper.[13] Search your heart for any such privately harbored anger. Name it, admit it, confess it, and put it away!

- *Second, do the Word*—James now moves to a "how-to": We are to lay aside all filthiness and overflow of wickedness—everything that soils us and whatever wickedness still remains in our heart, mind, and actions, and to welcome the seed of the Word with a humble heart. James's picture here is one of stripping off dirty, vile clothing. Is there any "filthiness" and evil that you need to deal with and eliminate from your life? Think through your normal daily schedule—what you watch, read, and think about, the people you listen to, and what they're talking about. We all live in the world and are exposed regularly to its "filthiness." Jot down two or three elements you want to strip off and get rid of.

(Just a note: Not only does God's Word bring us the truth that initially saves us from the penalty of sin, but it also guides us and guards us each and every day.)

And now James gives us a "do" to do: We are to be *doers* of the Word, and not hearers only.

Did you enjoy James's illustration of the man who looks in the mirror and does nothing about what he sees? Well then, maybe you'll enjoy this story, too!

*T*he story is told of an elderly man, very nearsighted, who took great pride in posing as a critic of art. One day he visited the art museum with some friends and immediately began to give his criticisms of the various paintings. Stopping before a full-length portrait, he began to take it apart. He had left his glasses at home and could not see the picture clearly. With an air of superiority he began: "The frame," said he, "is altogether out of keeping with the picture. The subject (a man) is too homely and shabbily dressed. In fact he is ugly, and it was a great mistake for the artist to select such a shoddy subject for his portrait." The old fellow was going on in this way, when his wife managed to get to him and pulling him aside, whispered in his ear, "My dear, you are looking in a mirror." [14]

Do you read God's Word with a seeking heart? It's a mirror, you know. In it we see ourselves as we really are—blemishes, faults, and all! Take an inventory, write out a list of any changes you need to make, and then commit them to God in prayer, asking for His grace and strength to "just do it!" (And don't forget the promise of God's blessing to the one who "does it!"—verse 25.)

- *Third, live the Word*—James now brings up several tests for truly living out the Word of God. They're practical and they're daily. In short, James says that if we think of ourselves as "religious" we must be sure that we...

...bridle our tongue. It's been estimated that "the average person will speak some 18,000 words in a day, enough for a fifty-four-page book. In a year that amounts to sixty-six 800-page volumes!...Up to one-fifth of the average person's life is spent talking."[15] Chart a plan for talking less! Determine at least three ways you will speak less. Plan a "fast"—a quiet time or a day of rest—for your tongue. (And be sure to include the elimination—by God's grace—of speech that is ungracious.)

...visit the orphans and widows in their distress. This means to care for those less fortunate than you who need others to look out for them. Are you acquainted with any people like this? How can you help or encourage them today, this week, and in the weeks to come so that it becomes a regular part of your "religion," of your faith lived out?

...keep ourselves unstained and unspotted by the world. We are *in* the world, but we are not *of* the world. Therefore, we're to live a godly lifestyle and keep ourselves untarnished and uncontaminated by the world. Since we're dealing in three's, name three practices you have control over that you know have an impure effect on your walk with the Lord. Then note what you will "do" to keep yourself pure from these influences.

1.

2.

3.

From the Heart of a Woman

Dear friend, in our previous lesson we witnessed the role of God's Word in our salvation, in giving us a new birth. And now here in this passage we learned that the Word of God not only produces regeneration, but is also an active force in our sanctification, in our purification. Why not accept James's challenges to obediently live out your life in Christ, which came about by the work of the Word, by means of the Word? Oh, the beauty of a woman after God's own heart who puts her faith into action and

controls her tongue,

changes her behavior on the outside to honor God, and carries out God's guidelines on the inside, in her heart!

Lesson 8

Dealing with Favoritism, Part 1

James 2:1-4

*H*ave you ever been on the negative end of favoritism? Snubbed with a haughty sneer? Ignored when you arrived at an event? Abruptly passed—even bumped out of the way—by another as she rushed to speak to someone else? Passed over by a group or a committee because you weren't as "sharp" as another woman?

We both know the pain of partiality. And what's worse is that we've also dished out plenty of partiality ourselves! It seems that no matter what our status is, there are always others who are better looking, wealthier, and more talented than we are...and there are always others who fall beneath us. It seems like we spend our whole life looking up at some and down on others.

Well, James definitely tells it the way it really is in our lesson today! He not only deals with those who are looking down on us, but he deals with us as we look up and down the scale of humanity, too.

But James also points us to a better—indeed, a "glorious"—standard. That standard is the one set by our Lord Jesus Christ, the Lord of glory, a standard of impartiality and equality.

As I said, we've got large lessons to learn! So whisper a prayer...and proceed!

James 2:1-4

1 My brethren, do not hold the faith of our Lord Jesus Christ, the Lord of glory, with partiality.

2 For if there should come into your assembly a man with gold rings, in fine apparel, and there should also come in a poor man in filthy clothes,

3 and you pay attention to the one wearing the fine clothes and say to him, "You sit here in a good place," and say to the poor man, "You stand there," or, "Sit here at my footstool,"

4 have you not shown partiality among yourselves, and become judges with evil thoughts?

God's Message...

1. What command does James make in verse 1?

To make his point, what two things does James say absolutely do *not* go together in a Christian (verse 1)?

a. b.

2. Through the use of a hypothetical situation, what contrasts does James use (verses 2-3)?

Man #1's dress—

Man #2's dress—

And what is Man #2 called (verse 2)?

In James's illustration, what is said to Man #1 (verse 3)?

And what is said to Man #2 (verse 3)?

3. What does James say his readers are doing when they think such things, speak such words, and treat different kinds of people in different ways (verse 4)?

4. It's always good to look at examples in the Bible, and in Malachi 2 we see God delivering a verdict against His priests through Malachi. Why? Because of favoritism. They had allowed certain people to break God's law and go unpunished. Read verses 8 and 9. What did Malachi say they had done wrong?

5. Note these instances of God's impartiality. Who did He bless, and how?

Matthew 5:43-45—

Luke 6:35—

...And Your Heart's Response

Partiality—meaning to favor one party more than the other and to be biased—was obviously a problem in the early church. And both you and I know that partiality is still a problem! Showing favoritism based on social standing is simply a part of our sinful nature. And James condemns such sinful preferences. Even more serious, he makes it a cause for questioning the reality of our faith.

This study is all about growing in wisdom and faith. So let's be sure we get the message about faith that God has for us through James, that we get it right and get it into practice.

- James begins his message to us with what two words (verse 1)?

He's speaking to the body of Christ. More specifically, the entire scenario is one of a church meeting. And you know that visitors often come to church. Again, when they do show up to visit, how does James say *not* to treat them (verse 1)?

Being partial or a respecter of persons has no place in the life of a believer toward whom God showed no partiality. What is the message of these scriptures?

Leviticus 19:15—

Deuteronomy 1:17—

Proverbs 24:23—

Proverbs 28:21—

Matthew 22:16—

- Next we saw James launch into a fictionalized (or was it?!) church meeting with two kinds of visitors—a rich "gold-fingered" man in fine, bright, gorgeous clothing, and a poor man in dirty, smelly clothes. James imagines that the wealthy man is warmly greeted and invited to sit in a special place of honor, while the vile visitor is pointed to a corner to stand in or, worse yet, to a place reserved for feet—a footstool.

Can you think of a time when someone unseemly showed up at your church service or Bible study? Jot down what you initially thought. In the end, how was the visitor treated?

Here's a question with quite an answer!

*W*hy is it wrong to show favoritism to the wealthy?

It is inconsistent with Christ's teachings.

It results from evil thoughts.

It belittles people made in God's image.

It is a by-product of selfish motives.

It goes against the biblical definition of love.

It shows a lack of mercy to those less fortunate.

It is hypocritical.

It is sin.[16]

- Take another moment to briefly answer this question: Toward what people or groups do you tend to show partiality?

What should your attitude be according to this passage from the Bible?

And how will you respond differently in the future?

Here's another bit of Bible teaching and theology to chew on. My pastor, Dr. John MacArthur, writes this about the character of God: "When we think of the attributes of God, His divine nature and characteristics, we usually think of such things as His holiness and righteousness and His omnipotence, omniscience, and omnipresence. We think of His immutability (changelessness), His eternality, His sovereignty, His justice, and His perfect grace, love, mercy, faithfulness, and goodness. *But another attribute of God that is not thought or spoken of so often is His impartiality.* Yet that is a serious and recurring theme throughout Scripture. God is absolutely impartial in His dealings with people. And in that way, as with His other attributes, He is unlike us" (emphasis added).[17]

From the Heart of a Woman

James's message is certainly clear, isn't it? We can't miss it! James warns us that we can neither be a woman after God's own heart nor a woman of faith if we "hold the faith of our Lord Jesus Christ, the Lord of glory," *and* treat anyone with partiality or favoritism. Such behavior is contradictory and incompatible with our salvation, a salvation which was accomplished by an impartial God, who showed no partiality toward us when we ourselves were vile sinners, but extended His love toward us...and died for us (see Romans 5:8).

As we leave this subject that we know all too well(!), pray through these questions. File them away in your heart. Their purpose is not to judge or to grade your church, but to see what it is *you*, dear one, can do. I'll be doing the exercise right along with you, and praying, too—for both of us!

§ How closely does your congregation reflect the socioeconomic and racial neighborhood in which you gather?

§ In your church, people may not be ushered to good or bad seats, but in what other ways might you be favoring the rich or discriminating against the poor?

§ Would a poor person feel welcome in your church? Would a rich person feel welcome in your church?

§ In what ways do you consciously or unconsciously favor some people over others in your church? Why do you do this?

§ How can your ministry reach out to all people without any hint of discrimination?

§ What can you do to be completely free from being impressed by the wealth or power of others?[18]

Lesson 9

Dealing with Favoritism, Part 2

James 2:5-13

The famed and eloquent preacher Dwight L. Moody wrote this note in his Bible's margin about the passage we're approaching. He noted, "The golden chain of obedience is broken if one link is missing."[19]

Favoritism—or partiality—my friend, is the area of disobedience that this section from James's epistle addresses. Continuing on from what he wrote previously on this subject (see Lesson 8), James meets the problem of partiality head on. And it's not a pretty sight! Using words that leave no doubt about their meaning, James writes, "...if you show partiality, you commit sin" (verse 9). In our last lesson, James got a good rolling start on this heinous sin of being a respecter of persons. But beware! He really presses his case here in these verses! James says, "Listen! Hearken! Pay attention!" Then he delivers an admonition aimed at the heart ("my beloved brethren") and at the mind (setting his case in perfect order so that his conclusions are obvious and easily understood).

As we look at our current lesson, keep Mr. Moody's astute words in mind—"The golden chain of obedience is broken if one link is missing." You'll be surprised to see how exacting he was in summarizing and illustrating James's message here in these verses!

And now, as James exhorts, listen....

James 2:5-13

⁵ Listen, my beloved brethren: Has God not chosen the poor of this world to be rich in faith and heirs of the kingdom which He promised to those who love Him?

⁶ But you have dishonored the poor man. Do not the rich oppress you and drag you into the courts?

⁷ Do they not blaspheme the noble name by which you are called?

⁸ If you really fulfill the royal law according to the Scripture, "You shall love your neighbor as yourself," you do well;

⁹ but if you show partiality, you commit sin, and are convicted by the law as transgressors.

¹⁰ For whoever shall keep the whole law, and yet stumble in one point, he is guilty of all.

¹¹ For He who said, "Do not commit adultery," also said, "Do not commit murder." Now if you do not commit adultery, but you do murder, you have become a transgressor of the law.

[12] So speak and so do as those who will be judged by the law of liberty.

[13] For judgment is without mercy to the one who has shown no mercy. Mercy triumphs over judgment.

God's Message...

1. God's message through James is about the "poor" and the "rich." To begin our observations, how does *God* view the poor (verse 5)?

   a.   b.

   And, in a word, what does James say partiality and low estimation of the poor communicates (verse 6)?

2. According to James, what was the general truth about the rich in relation to his readers?

   a.   (Verse 6)—

   b.   (Verse 6)—

   c.   (Verse 7)—

3. In verse 8 James states "the royal law" according to the Scriptures. What is it?

   And what is the opposite of the royal law (verse 9)?

4. As James reasons with his readers, he writes that…

...if you fulfill the royal law, you_____
(verse 8), but…

...if you do not fulfill the royal law and show partiality,
you_____ (verse 9).

5. What is the result of stumbling and offending in even
one (including showing partiality and favoritism) point
of the whole law (verse 10)?

And what will happen to the one who shows no mercy
(verse 13)?

…and Your Heart's Response

- *The royal law*—What does Matthew tell us the royal law
is (see Matthew 22:37-40)?

a.

b.

- *Love*—Now briefly note what Paul had to say about love
(see Romans 13:8-10).

And, of course, we're *most* interested in what Jesus had to say about love (see John 13:34)!

Long before these New Testament references to the royal law, what did God's Law have to say?

Deuteronomy 6:5—

Leviticus 19:18—

- Our study from James is about growing in wisdom and faith, and we're considering his instructions to us for being women of faith. Look again at James's teachings in verses 5-13 about the sin of favoritism. In your own words, write a few sentences about *why* James is so fervent in his message to us. (He's now gone on about it for 13 verses!)

- Finally, how does James say God treats the poor (verse 5)?

How, then, can you show mercy to the poor? Think of several real ways you can extend your hand to the poor and to the needy (Proverbs 31:20). When you love and honor the poor, dear one, you distinguish yourself as a woman after God's own heart!

From the Heart of a Woman

It was Abraham Lincoln who said, "God must love the common people because He made so many of them!"[20] As I'm meditating on James's words, I'm thinking about the many poor "common people" in the Bible that were "rich in faith and heirs of the kingdom which [God] promised to those who love Him." May I leave you with this partial-but-powerful list? Let's learn from them about a heart of faith!

> ❧ The widow of Zarephath—had no one to care for her and was so poor she was preparing her last bite to eat before she and her son would lie down and wait to die. Yet this rich-in-faith, poor-in-means woman later declared her faith (1 Kings 17).
>
> ❧ Ruth and Naomi—were also destitute widows...until God sent Boaz to honor their faith and to care for them (Ruth 2).
>
> ❧ Anna—yet another widow, lived out her great faith as she served God with fastings and prayers night and day in the temple (Luke 2:37).
>
> ❧ Paul—the Lord's apostle to the Gentiles, learned to be content and trust in the Lord when he was abased, hungry, and without the bare necessities (Philippians 4:11-12).
>
> ❧ And our dear Jesus—the One who is Faithful and True, had no place to lay His head (Matthew 8:20).

Surely it is better to be rich in faith than rich in funds!

Lesson 10

Showing Forth Your Faith

ne principle of good Bible study is to pay attention to the amount of space a writer spends on a particular topic. And dear James just can't seem to let go of the snubbing and mistreatment of the poor. As we noted in our previous lesson, James has been at it for 13 verses already, and now he adds four more! Like a builder who hammers away on his nail until it sinks deeply and completely into the wood, James keeps his sure blows coming. Sooner or later his readers (and we, too!) will surely get the message!

And, like a masterful carpenter, James here reaches into his bag and pulls out yet another nail to drive into the structure of his treatise against showing favoritism toward the rich while shunning the poor. We can almost imagine James hitting the nail just a little harder with each driving question he asks. Let's allow his queries to impact us, too.

James 2:14-17

¹⁴ What does it profit, my brethren, if someone says he has faith but does not have works? Can faith save him?

¹⁵ If a brother or sister is naked and destitute of daily food,

¹⁶ and one of you says to them, "Depart in peace, be warmed and filled," but you do not give them the things which are needed for the body, what does it profit?

¹⁷ Thus also faith by itself, if it does not have works, is dead.

God's Message...

1. James sets about to contrast the words and works of his readers. What does the man in verse 14 *say*?

And yet what is missing from his life (verse 14)?

And what searing question does James have for this man (verse 14)?

So far, James has asked two of his three questions. And for your information, the answers to his questions call for an expected, resounding NOTHING! and NO!

2. Next, James gives a "for instance," an example, of faith without *works*. What is the condition of the poor person in need (verse 15)?

And what is the verbal response, the *words*, of the person who observes these conditions (verse 16)?

a.   b.   c.

And what does he *do*?

Utterly amazed, James asks (verse 16)…

3. What is James's conclusion to *words* without *works*, to talk without action, to profession of faith without performance of the deeds of faith (verse 17)?

…and Your Heart's Response

James 2:17 is considered by most scholars and teachers of the Bible to be the key verse to the book of James. Why don't you write it out here? (Memorize it, too!)

- It's important to understand that the faith James is talking about here is a so-called or fake faith. How can we tell? Because of 1) the statement, "if someone says he has faith" and 2) the definitive word *that* in James's statement, "can *that* faith save him?" (verse 14 NASB). According to one reference volume…

    It is only a false faith that does not issue in works and that is incapable of saving. By *works* James does not have in mind the Jewish doctrine of works as a means of salvation, but rather works of faith, the ethical outworking of true piety and especially the "work of love" (James 2:8).[21]

In the example James gives of a needy, poor person, what would the "work of love" or the works of true faith do?

- Can you think of ways you can show forth your faith and let your love shine toward the needy? As you answer, consider again James's advice in James 1:27.

- As a close-to-home application, take a look at your own family members. Oh, they're probably not "naked and destitute of daily food," but they do need clean, warm clothing and three meals a day from you! How can you show your works of true faith and do the works of love right under your own roof this week (...and with a heart of love, too)?

- Here's a subject for prayer. As Paul pleaded with the Corinthians, "Examine yourselves as to whether you are in the faith. Prove yourselves" (2 Corinthians 13:5). Examine your own faith, dear one. As the familiar question charges, "Is there enough 'evidence' (or, are there enough good works) to convict you of being a Christian?" You may want to jot down any serious resolutions here.

From the Heart of a Woman

And speaking of prayer, I've prayed about whether or not to share with you the following. I admit, it's scathing! But, then, so is James's outrage at withholding from the poor while honoring those who prosper. So, let's allow one more voice to admonish us about practical Christianity.

What an illustration [verses 15-16] and how practical. What this poor, naked, hungry brother or sister needs is clothing and food. Pious prayers will not help him. Reading Scripture to him will not clothe him. Speaking kind words will not feed him and make him warm. He needs clothes and food and if you are in a position to furnish them, then don't shirk your duty by saying to the poor brother, "We'll pray for you and God will supply your need." You hypocrite, you cover up your penurious, stingy heart and clamp down your fist upon your purse by offering prayers instead of clothing, and pious talk instead of food. Listen! That is what is wrong today....The world wants action, not words, and many a cheap, stingy heart is camouflaged under pious cant and hollow prayer. The world is not interested in our prayers. It wants evidence.

...God help us...[to] strive until our faith has been demonstrated before men and we are justified before the world by the life we live and the works we do.

"Giving is living," the angel said,

"God fed the hungry sweet charity's bread!"

"And must I keep giving and giving again?"

My selfish and querulous answer ran...

"Oh, no," said the angel, his eyes pierced me through,

"Just give till the Saviour stops giving to you!"

—Anonymous.[22]

Lesson 11

Working Out Your Faith

I once heard a pastor tell a story about making a deposit at one of his bank's regional branches. His wife had told him exactly where the bank branch was located. In fact, she even wrote it down for him—go to the small building in the northeast corner of the parking lot at the local mall. Well, when he got there, he found that the bank wasn't theirs but was another bank. When he got home that evening, they had quite a discussion over dinner, each insisting that he and she was right! So they got in the car and drove to the mall to settle their dispute…only to find that they were both right! The building in the parking lot housed two banks! All those years, the wife had never noticed the other bank's entrance on the opposite side of the structure, which just happened to be the side her husband drove up to, never seeing their bank on the other end. They were both right!

That's a nice way to settle a disagreement, isn't it? To discover that you're both right?

And, dear one, that's what's happening in the book of James. Here in this lesson, we run into what many consider to be the most difficult section in the letter. Are you wondering why? Well, it has to do with the role that "works" (the resultant fruit of genuine faith) play in evidencing genuine faith (which is accomplished by Christ apart from any works). The apostle Paul emphasized justification by faith apart from works (Romans 4) while James here in Chapter 2 emphasizes the fact that true saving faith will be accompanied by works. Many have seen this as a contradiction between these two giants in the Church. But, just like the man and wife who were each right about the bank, Paul and James are both right in their assessment of faith and works. They're not in disagreement. They're simply looking at faith and works from two different angles, proving two different points.

Let's look now at James's point of view.

James 2:18-26

18 But someone will say, "You have faith, and I have works." Show me your faith without your works, and I will show you my faith by my works.

19 You believe that there is one God. You do well. Even the demons believe—and tremble!

20 But do you want to know, O foolish man, that faith without works is dead?

21 Was not Abraham our father justified by works when he offered Isaac his son on the altar?

22 Do you see that faith was working together with his works, and by works faith was made perfect?

²³ And the Scripture was fulfilled which says, "Abraham believed God, and it was accounted to him for righteousness." And he was called the friend of God.

²⁴ You see then that a man is justified by works, and not by faith only.

²⁵ Likewise, was not Rahab the harlot also justified by works when she received the messengers and sent them out another way?

²⁶ For as the body without the spirit is dead, so faith without works is dead also.

God's Message...

1. James imagines the objections or questions his far away readers might have to what he's saying about faith and the necessity of works. One objection had to do with their belief in the basic teaching of Judaism, that God is one. Write out Deuteronomy 6:4 here:

Who else believes in the one God, and what effect does it have on them (James 2:19)?

2. Another objection was their relationship with their Jewish "father," Abraham. Using two different illustrations of two different people from two different walks of life, James points out the works of each that proved their faith.

One is *Abraham*, a man, a leader, a father, and the father of the Jewish nation. Of Abraham, James writes in verse 21,

"Was not Abraham our father justified by works when… (fill in the rest)…

Scan through the account of Abraham's "work of faith" in Genesis 22:1-14. According to Genesis 22:12, what did Abraham's "work of faith" prove?

The second illustration used by James is Rahab, a woman, "a nobody," a single, and a prostitute. Of Rahab, James writes in verse 25, "Likewise, was not Rahab the harlot also justified by works when…(fill in the rest)…"

Now scan through the account of Rahab's "work of faith" in Joshua 2:1-16. What was Rahab's great "work of faith" (see Joshua 2:3-4, 15-16)?

3. Twice James uses the word "dead"—once in a statement and once in his conclusion. What is his statement (verse 20)?

And what is his conclusion (verse 26)?

…and Your Heart's Response

- To learn more about what the Bible says about "faith" and "works," see what these scriptures have to say:

Galatians 5:6—

Ephesians 2:8-10—

Titus 3:5—

Titus 3:8—

1 John 3:18—

Just to summarize, how then are we saved?

And what is the visible evidence of genuine faith?

- James had come to his conclusions about faith and works. Hopefully the readers of his letter also came to the same conclusion. But what is most important to know is, what is *your* conclusion (verse 26)?

- Both Abraham and Rahab took costly risks where the proof of their faith was concerned. What has been the proof of your faith this last week?

From the Heart of a Woman

How does one become a woman of faith? When I read of the faith of Abraham and of Rahab, I marvel! Where did their faith come from? How was it nurtured? How was it strengthened? And how can I do the same?

I decided that I would search for answers to these questions and share them here.

Question 1: Where does faith come from? The answer, in a word, is *grace*, God's *grace*. In Ephesians 2:8-10 (which we looked at just above), we learn that by *grace* we are saved. And, dear one, even that *grace* is a *grace*-gift of God and not of ourselves! Faith, then, is a work of God in our hearts.

Question 2: How is faith nurtured and strengthened? Here are a few sure ways:

a) *By reading the Word.* When we read the Bible, we're allowed to walk hand in hand with the giants of faith. We can see up close the trials and testings and temptations they faced and how they faced each with faith. Sometimes we even get to see how they failed! We can enter into their struggles, see what they did, and hear what they said. We can also read what God says about faith, like here in James 2.

b) *By hearing the Word.* God has given His church another kind of gift—gifted teachers—to help us grow in faith (Ephesians 4:11). Hearing the Bible taught and expounded and explained fuels our faith.

Here's a final thought—*Be sharing the Word.* Paul tells us that "...faith comes by hearing, and hearing by the word of God" (Romans 10:17). As you and I are faithful to share the gospel, the Good News of Jesus Christ, and the faith that we enjoy, others can respond to it.

(And don't forget—we're not only to tell the Word and to take the Word to others. We're also to back up the Word with our works. So, besides sharing the gospel with someone, think of something you can also *do* for that person. That way you send a double message about your faith!)

Lesson 12

Speaking with Wisdom

Some unknown person (who seems to have understood the meaning of James 3:1-4 well!) wrote that "He who teaches the Bible is never a scholar; he is always a student." It's been said by someone that "there are two dangers which every teacher must avoid.... He must have every care that he is teaching the truth, and not his own opinions or even his own prejudices. It is fatally easy for a teacher to distort the truth and to teach, not God's version, but his own. He must [also] have every care that he does not contradict his teaching by his life...."[23]

These are sobering words—and warnings—for us as we're seeking to grow in wisdom, in faith, and in the knowledge of the truth.

Well, as we've seen all along the way, James, too, is a man of sobering words and warnings. And he not only has a few words for us here about the use of the tongue to teach the Word of God, but also has application for the use of speech in general.

James 3:1-4

¹ My brethren, let not many of you become teachers, knowing that we shall receive a stricter judgment.

² For we all stumble in many things. If anyone does not stumble in word, he is a perfect man, able also to bridle the whole body.

³ Indeed, we put bits in horses' mouths that they may obey us, and we turn their whole body.

⁴ Look also at ships: although they are so large and are driven by fierce winds, they are turned by a very small rudder wherever the pilot desires.

God's Message...

Warnings. That's what this passage in James is about. And, as we learned above, he has two for his readers—including us. At the base of each warning is the use of the tongue.

1. James's first warning is directed at whom (verse 1)?

    What does James say awaits this category of people (verse 1)?

2. Next, James moves from "teachers" (verse 1) to "all" (verse 2). What general statement does he make (verse 2a)?

And how does he define a perfect man (verse 2b)?

What does James say a person who controls his tongue is also able to do (verse 2)?

3. Ever the illustrator, James now uses two illustrations from life. What are they?

Verse 3—   Verse 4—

What can one small human do to control the first (verse 3)?

And what can one small human do to control the second (verse 4)?

...and Your Heart's Response

- In our first few lessons, we noted the problems James's readers faced and their faulty understanding of God and of other areas of theology. James wrote this letter to correct their wrong thinking and understanding. And now here in this passage he sets about to correct those who are teaching such things. What advice does Paul have for teachers in Romans 2:21-22?

- What advice does Paul have for us as women in Titus 2:3?

  According to Paul in Titus 2:4-5, what are some of the "good things" we are to teach to other women?

What instruction can we gain from the Proverbs 31 woman in Proverbs 31:26 about how we are to teach?

If you are, or think you want to be, a teacher of God's truth, be sure to ask yourself, "Why?" Why do you want to be a teacher? What are your motives? And are they free from selfish ambitions?

- Sometimes the best lessons are taught with a quiet tongue! What do these verses from the Bible have to say about silence versus harmful words?

Proverbs 12:18—

Proverbs 15:2—

Proverbs 15:28—

- By now we know how difficult it is to control the tongue. Indeed, James says it's easier to control a powerful horse with a bit in its mouth or a wind-driven sailing vessel with a small rudder than it is to control our tongue! Think through the use of your tongue during the past few days. How would you categorize your words? Was your speech soft (Proverbs 15:1)? Were your words true (Proverbs 12:22)? Did they bring "health" to the hearer (Proverbs 16:24)? Why not write out a few decisions about your own tongue and your use of it?

Hear this prayer from the heart of King David: "Let the words of my mouth and the meditation of my heart be acceptable in Your sight, O Lord, my strength and my redeemer" (Psalm 19:14). How do you think this prayer—and an earnest desire to please God—could help you with your mouth?

From the Heart of a Woman

It's a good idea for us to pause right here as we're contemplating teaching and teachers and remember those who have faithfully and accurately taught us. Indeed, they take a great risk (in light of James 3:1) each and every time they open their mouth. As James says, theirs is the stricter judgment!

Think first of your pastor. Thank God for his diligent study, that he seeks to rightly divide God's Word and to cut it straight (2 Timothy 2:15).

And think of your parents who imparted to you skills, values, and instruction for life. And, if they're Christians, think of how they introduced you to God, to His Son, and to the Bible. No matter what, we all have *something* that our parents have taught us that we can thank the Lord for.

And think, too, of school teachers and professors, who, like the candle, light others by consuming themselves. God has used these dedicated souls to enlighten our lives.

And especially think of those you consider to be your "older women" (Titus 2:3), the ones who unselfishly take (or have taken) time to share with you, to encourage you, to instruct you, and to train you in the "good things" of the Lord! What I would be without a corps of these lovers of my soul, I don't know! Thank God that these dear saints put their tongues to good use!

And now, please join me as I pray that you and I will both speak with wisdom, that we may each use our tongue to be a light to others who struggle in darkness, that we may possess "the tongue of the learned" so that we might freely give a word of encouragement and instruction to those who are weary (Isaiah 50:4). Amen!

Lesson 13

Taming the Tongue

Oh, those junior high school pastors! They must certainly be a unique breed! But we definitely owe them a tremendous debt. When we as parents reach our wits' end at home trying to train up our young teens, behold! We send them off to their youth meeting, and somehow that terrific junior high pastor gets through to them!

Yes, they are unique…and they have some unique ways of delivering their messages that impacts adolescents. Here's what my two junior high daughters shared with Jim and me one Wednesday night after their youth group.

The youth pastor was teaching through James and had arrived at this passage in James 3 about the tongue. Earlier that day he had gone to the grocery store and purchased a two-pound cow tongue. Then, while he taught about how ugly the tongue is and the damage an unguarded tongue can do, he passed the cow tongue around so each teen could look at it and touch it! I don't have to tell you the indelible impression this "visual aid" made on my girls! They've never forgotten that particular lesson...and neither have I.

Unfortunately, the tongue is ugly, "a world of iniquity," says James, adding that it is "set on fire by hell" and "an unruly evil, full of deadly poison." That's awful, isn't it? And frightening, too! So hearken carefully to what James has to say to us about taming the tongue.

James 3:5-8

⁵ Even so the tongue is a little member and boasts great things. See how great a forest a little fire kindles!

⁶ And the tongue is a fire, a world of iniquity. The tongue is so set among our members that it defiles the whole body, and sets on fire the course of nature; and it is set on fire by hell.

⁷ For every kind of beast and bird, of reptile and creature of the sea, is tamed and has been tamed by mankind.

⁸ But no man can tame the tongue. It is an unruly evil, full of deadly poison.

God's Message...

1. James uses a string of descriptions for the tongue and its activities. See if you can pick them out.

   Verse 5 (look for two)—

Verse 6 (look for five)—

Verse 8 (look for two)—

2. What information does James share with us from nature in verse 7?

And what contrast does he present in verse 8?

3. Since the tongue can't be tamed, what is Paul's advice on controlling the tongue in Ephesians 4:29 and Titus 3:2?

...and Your Heart's Response

• James likens the tongue to a fire that is capable of burning down a great forest. For a bit of personal application, what do Proverbs 26:20 and Proverbs 16:27 say about the tongue that kindles fires?

Think of several ways you can ensure that you are not a part of such destruction.

• In our previous lesson we looked at being teachers of good things. Specifically, we looked at a passage instructing the older women on their roles within the church. Look again at Titus 2:3. What is said there about the speech patterns of these godly older women?

*I*n his book *The Measure of a Woman,* Dr. Gene Getz writes about "Three Categories of Gossip" in reference to James, Chapter 3:

*T*he first kind of gossip is malicious gossip. This is what James is talking about. Malicious gossip is consciously and deliberately hurtful. It is based in envy and rooted in flagrant selfishness. It is designed to break up relationships and destroy friendships. And it can manifest itself in all kinds of evil deeds.

*T*he second kind of gossip is rationalization. It is far more subtle than malicious gossip. What makes rationalization so dangerous is that it often results from self-deception. Rooted and based in the same motives as malicious gossip, the person who rationalizes has convinced herself (himself) that she is doing it for "the good" of the other person. She may disguise it as "prayer interest" and "personal concern." Nevertheless rationalization is very destructive.

*T*he third kind of gossip is "innocent" gossip. This involves a person who truly is concerned, but who is, to a certain extent, unwise and insensitive to other people's feelings. Innocent gossip is sometimes motivated by a desire to be "helpful," but in reality, the gossiper may be trying to prove to others "how helpful she really is." In this situation there is a very fine line between "selfish" and "unselfish" motives. All Christians must beware of this kind of gossip.[24]

Evaluate your talk about others against these three measuring sticks. Also evaluate who it is you tend to talk about and why. In which category do you fall? And what kinds of "radical surgery" (see Matthew 5:29-30) could you perform to eliminate this "unruly evil"? List at least three practices you can put into effect *today!*

From the Heart of a Woman

Have you ever been the "victim" of any of these three kinds of gossip, my friend? I'm almost certain that you have...and so have I. And, even worse, you, like me, have probably participated in all three yourself! My heart is sick as I recall my own pain and my own part in the pain I've surely caused others, especially our dear Lord who died for these sins.

As I write this lesson, it's winter. And last week the television news carried a sad interview with the victims of a house fire. Dirty from the ordeal of escape, wide-eyed from leftover terror, and sobbing in desperation, the couple (with their little ones hugging their legs) shared words like these— "We lost everything we had." "I don't know what we'll do." "We have to start all over again." "Everything's gone that we've worked so hard for!"

I'm sickened again. Why? Because this is exactly what we do with our tongue when we ravage someone with our vicious, malicious words, when we reveal a vile heart through gossip and slander. When we're finished and the damage is done, the poor people we've harmed are left dirty from the ordeal, wide-eyed from the horror of it, and sobbing in desperation, "I've lost everything I had—my good name, my reputation, my standing." "I don't know what I'll do—my name's been smeared." "I have to start all over again—building my reputation."

As James writes, "See how great a forest a little fire kindles!" Oh, dear one, do whatever you have to do to tame your tongue, to build instead of destroy, to encourage instead of annihilate, to minister instead of massacre with your tongue!

Lesson 14

Blessing…or Cursing?

James 3:9-12

efore we move on to yet another(!) study about the words that proceed out of our mouth, I wanted to pass on this bit of encouraging advice I found in my reading. James said and summarized, and I quote, "…no man can tame the tongue" (James 3:8). Before you get too discouraged and give up, read on…

> If no human being can control the tongue, why bother trying? Because even if we do not achieve perfect control of it in this life, we can still learn enough control to reduce the damage it can do. It is better to fight a fire than to go around setting new ones! Remember that we are not fighting the tongue's fire in our own strength. The Holy Spirit

> will give us increasing power to monitor and control what we say. As Christians we are not perfect, but we should never stop growing.... God works to change us from the inside out. As the Holy Spirit purifies our hearts, he also gives us self-control so that we will speak words that please God.[25]

I hope it comforts you to know that there is hope in the Holy Spirit! And now, let's move on.

Most appliances have only one use. A can opener is for opening cans. A vacuum cleaner is for cleaning. An oven is for cooking.

But when it comes to the tongue, James is appalled! He's flabbergasted! Why? Because he sees it used in such opposing ways.

Hear now the heart of James on the matter of the incredible tongue!

James 3:9-12

[9] With it we bless our God and Father, and with it we curse men, who have been made in the similitude of God.

[10] Out of the same mouth proceed blessing and cursing. My brethren, these things ought not to be so.

[11] Does a spring send forth fresh water and bitter from the same opening?

[12] Can a fig tree, my brethren, bear olives, or a grapevine bear figs? Thus no spring can yield both salt water and fresh.

God's Message...

1. What inconsistencies does James marvel at in verse 9?

   And in verse 10?

   Of what fact about mankind does James remind us (verse 9)?

2. What conclusive remark does he make regarding these inconsistencies (verse 10)?

3. To bring his message home to his readers (and that includes us), James again illustrates from nature. List the four instances he uses to prove how awful and unnatural the behavior of the tongue can be:

   Verse 11 (look for one)—

   Verse 12 (look for three)—

...and Your Heart's Response

- Read verse 9 again. How does this verse reinforce James's earlier statement regarding partiality?

  How do you generally view others, and how does James's statement here about "similitude" or likeness "correct" your view?

(Just a note—When James speaks of blessing God with our mouths, his Jewish readers probably took notice because every time God's name was mentioned, they were required to bless Him with the words, "Blessed be He!" In fact, devout Jews were required three times a day to repeat 18 prayers called *Eulogies*, each began with the words, "Blessed be thou, O God." God was "The Blessed One" and was to be continually blessed.)

- As you consider James's questions from nature, what answer do you think he expects?

And why can he expect such an answer?

James is reasoning with his readers. What do you think his purpose is? Or, put another way, what does he want them to understand?

- Look at God's high calling for His women in 1 Timothy 3:11. This verse is in a passage that describes ministry within the church and those who minister there. What does this verse say about the speech of the women who serve in the church?

- Now look again at God's high calling for His women in Titus 2:3. Again, this passage defines the roles of the different age groups within the church. What does this verse say about the speech of the older women who serve in the church?

And to what good use were they to put their mouths to instead (Titus 2:3-4)?

Why do you think the women who were to instruct and encourage the young women in the church were not to be slanderers and gossips?

• In view of these high callings from God, what will you do to change and channel your speech patterns and the use of your mouth?

From the Heart of a Woman

Blessing...or cursing? That's the question James raises here about our own speech, dear friend! Before we leave this awful subject (and one James has now spent twelve verses on!), I do want to share some shocking information that turned my life around in this all-important area of the tongue. And that was learning about the source of gossip!

Did you know that the word *gossip* is used in the Bible for the devil himself? His very name is *diabolos*, "slanderer." In fact, "slanderer" is used 34 times in Scripture as a title for Satan and once to refer to Judas, the one who betrayed our Jesus (John 6:70). This is frightening company, and no woman who loves God and whom He calls to serve His women in the church should be a gossip or a slanderer, or more literally, a "she-devil"! We know that Jesus taught that the devil is a liar and the father of lies (John 8:44). Sadly, when we participate in gossip and slander we're acting like the devil, the accuser of the brethren (Revelation 12:10) and our adversary who walks about like a roaring lion, seeking whom he may devour (1 Peter 5:8).

Blessing...or cursing? Won't you make a choice to bless God and man with the fruit of your lips?

Lesson 15

Defining True Wisdom

James 3:13-18

I'm excited we're approaching this passage from James 3. Verse 17 could well be my favorite verse in the epistle of James. It so clearly describes the special beauty of the fruit of wisdom and its rare fragrances of humility and gentleness, indeed, a life of lovely graciousness. It's presented to us by James as sort of a checklist. We'll go through the many positive blessings that godly words of wisdom bring to its hearers, but first let's look over these six verses from James.

James 3:13-18

¹³ Who is wise and understanding among you? Let him show by good conduct that his works are done in the meekness of wisdom.

¹⁴ But if you have bitter envy and self-seeking in your hearts, do not boast and lie against the truth.

¹⁵ This wisdom does not descend from above, but is earthly, sensual, demonic.

¹⁶ For where envy and self-seeking exist, confusion and every evil thing will be there.

¹⁷ But the wisdom that is from above is first pure, then peaceable, gentle, willing to yield, full of mercy and good fruits, without partiality and without hypocrisy.

¹⁸ Now the fruit of righteousness is sown in peace by those who make peace.

God's Message...

1. Look back at James 3, verse 1, and note who James was addressing before digressing to include everyone.

2. To turn his message back to the original group of teachers he was addressing in James 3:1, what question does James skillfully pose (verse 13)?

And what exhortation does he have for them (verse 13)?

Try putting verse 13 into your own words.

Suddenly "wisdom" is reintroduced. It's been a while since James has dealt with this topic (see James 1:5). Yet here he begins a detailed contrast between two kinds of wisdom. Complete the following chart for a better understanding.

The wisdom that is *not* from above...

Its source (verse 15)	Its motivation (verse 14)	Its product (verse 16)
a.	a.	a
b.	b.	b.
c.		

What eight qualities describe the wisdom that *is* from above (verse 17)?

a.	e.
b.	f.
c.	g.
d.	h.

...and Your Heart's Response

As you work your way through James's own words of wisdom, consider these definitions and explanations of the eight components of true spiritual wisdom, the kind that comes down from above.

- *Pure*—true wisdom is free from all ulterior motives and self-interest.

How do you think faithfulness in your prayer life could help bring about greater purity?

- *Peaceable*—true wisdom accomplishes peace in relationships, whether with another person or with God.

- *Gentle*—true wisdom is forgiving and extends kindness and consideration to all.

Share what Paul had to say about this quality in 2 Timothy 2:24:

- *Willing to yield*—true wisdom is marked by a willingness to listen and a sense of knowing when to yield to the proper standards.

On this matter, see Proverbs 18:13:

- *Full of mercy*—true wisdom reaches out to help others.

Jesus had something to say on this mark of divine wisdom in Matthew 5:7:

- *Full of good fruits*—true wisdom bears the "good fruits" of every sort of action and practical assistance.

Jot down some of these good fruits from Galatians 5:22-23:

- *Without partiality*—true wisdom does not waver or vacillate in indecision nor play favorites in dispensing truth and holding to its standard.

  Read again James 2:1-9! He's had plenty to say about partiality! What is his final verdict in verse 9?

- *Without hypocrisy*—true wisdom does not deal in deception, pretension, or selfishness.

  According to Peter in 1 Peter 2:1 what are we to do with hypocrisy? (Also don't forget to notice the company it keeps!)

- How are you doing on this checklist, dear growing woman of wisdom and faith? Are these "good fruits" evident in your life? Or did you find any of these marks of wisdom missing from your lips and life? Jot them down here or circle them above.

  Think a moment about your relationships and your effect on others. Are you a sower of peace? Are you a peacemaker to all you come in contact with? Are you a promoter of peace and righteousness?

- Finally, for any shortcomings in wisdom...

  ...look first at God's list of causes in verses 14-16 and pinpoint any sin...

...then look at the Bible reference that accompanies each sterling quality of wisdom. Ask God to guide you in supplying any missing elements of wisdom.

From the Heart of a Woman

I know this lesson has gone a little long, but I'm sure you agree that it's been extremely rich. May yours be a heart of wisdom, dear one. May your words be those of wisdom. And may your prayer echo that of Charles Spurgeon, widely esteemed master of theology and of the pulpit, regarding James 1:13: "Grant, most precious God, that I may never hold so high an opinion of my own spiritual health as to prevent my being in my deeds full of your grace and fear!"[26]

Lesson 16

Looking at Your Heart

James 4:1-3

War and peace. I know these words make up the title of a classic novel, but they also describe two conditions in the church. In our previous lesson, James left us on the gracious subject of peace and the sweet fruits of righteousness that peace bears in the body of Christ.

But James seesaws here. Previously he wrote about the subjects of disorderly conduct, envy, and every evil thing (James 3:14-16). Then he dwelt on the opposite of such ugliness—on peace and peacemaking (James 3:17-18). Now James turns his pen once again to strife and contention and conflict. He asks boldly where such awful actions come from! His answer to his own question will teach us much about the problem of strife and God's solution to the problem.

As we peer into this pit of dark deeds, remember what one gentleman wisely noted—

> The ladder that leads down to hell has three steps; on the first, there is written "earthly"; on the second, "sensual"; and down there, just at hell's door comes the third, and on it is written "devilish."[27]

James 4:1-3

1 Where do wars and fights come from among you? Do they not come from your desires for pleasure that war in your members?

2 You lust and do not have. You murder and covet and cannot obtain. You fight and war. Yet you do not have because you do not ask.

3 You ask and do not receive, because you ask amiss, that you may spend it on your pleasures.

God's Message...

1. What is obviously happening among the readers of James's letter (verse 1)?

2. There's a progression of sin presented here by James. To begin with, what does James say the source of the wars and fights among Christians is (verse 1)?

Then what happens when we lust and do not have (verse 2)?

And what happens when we are covetous and cannot obtain (verse 2)?

3. List two reasons James cites for not having a life of peace and satisfaction:

Verse 2—

Verse 3—

...and Your Heart Response

As we look more closely at our heart, these terms will help us grow in our understanding of sin and evil and of problems and solutions.

- *Wars*—James's first word to us is a Greek word used in a literal sense for armed conflict and in a figurative sense for strife, conflict, or quarreling. Evidently the sharp "weapon" of the tongue was doing its damage among James's readers! This picture of warring suggests a continuing state of hostility.

- *Fights*—Here we have more of the same—battles, quarrels, and disputes. The picture here is one of specific outbursts of hostility and antagonism. What outburst(s) of hostility does James mention in verse 2?

- *Desires for pleasure*—James now begins to put his finger on the causes of warring and fighting. He says the problem is inside—inside the heart where the selfish desire to fulfill every personal pleasure and passion festers. What bottom-line statement does Paul make about the love of pleasure in 2 Timothy 3:3-4?

- *Lust*—Lust is a desire or longing of any kind. And because lust cannot bring about inward peace, it results in unrest and discontent which then spills over onto others. What did James say earlier about lust in chapter 1, verse 14? And what did John say about lust in 1 John 2:15-16?

- *Murder*—The craving for pleasure and the inability to achieve it drives men to shameful deeds, even to murder and murderous hatred and attitudes. How did lust lead to murder in 1 Kings 21:1-14?

  What did Jesus consider to be murder in Matthew 5:21-22?

- *Covet*—It's easy to see how unchecked and uncontrolled desires can lead to extreme violence...even murder. In a few words, how did lust and coveting lead to murder in 2 Samuel 11:2-15?

*J*ames's references to wars and fighting led someone to come up with this clever list of "weapons and strategies used in church fights and quarrels." It's almost too true to chuckle over!

> Missiles—Attacking church members from long range.
>
> Guerrilla tactics—Ambushing the unsuspecting.
>
> Snipers—Well-aimed criticisms.
>
> Terrorism—No one is immune from being hurt.
>
> Mines—Ensuring that others will fail in their efforts to serve God.
>
> Espionage—Using friendships to get potentially damaging information about others.
>
> Propaganda—Using gossip to spread damaging information about others.
>
> Cold war—Freezing out an opponent by withdrawing or refusing to talk to him or her.
>
> Nuclear attack—Being willing to sacrifice the church if the goals of my group are not met.

James tells us the exact location of the manufacturing plants for all these weapons: The trouble is in ourselves.[28]

From the Heart of a Woman

Prayer has been called many things. "Fellowship with a holy God." "The greater work." "The most important thing in life." "The gymnasium of the soul." "The barometer of our spiritual condition." "The doorway into the secret place of the Most High." Certainly prayer is all of these things...and more!

Oh, sweet prayer! What a wholesome relief from James's ghastly list of sins to come to the matter of prayer. But it does come with a word of warning and instruction. First, there's a "right" way to pray and a "wrong" way. The wrong way to pray is not to pray at all! May we never be guilty of simply not praying! May we ever err on the side of more instead of less—or not at all—when it comes to prayer!

Another "wrong" way to pray is to ask for the wrong things. James says we are not to ask for things in order to consume them on our pleasures, to waste them upon our lustful desires.

Then there's asking for the "wrong" reasons. Be sure to lift your motives before the Lord, to take a look at your heart when you bring your requests before Him. And be willing to acknowledge your sinful motives and adjust them to match up with God's good and acceptable and perfect will, with what He tells us in His Word is pleasing to Him and right in His eyes. Prayer, dear one, is the beginning of the solution to the problem of strife!

So...take a long look at your heart. As a woman after God's own heart, you'll want to be sure to—

§   *Put a guard on your speech*—Proverbs 31:26
§   *Put away all bitterness and wrath*—Ephesians 4:31
§   *Put on a heart of prayer*—Philippians 1:3-7
§   *Put on a gentle and quiet spirit*—1 Peter 3:4

Lesson 17

Growing in Grace

Small things. We think they don't matter. We think there's no harm. We think there's no way something so small could hurt us at all. It's just *one* TV program. It's just *one* friend who's a little on the edge. It's just *one* date with an unbeliever. It's just *one* (more!) small expenditure. Yet one small thing can be one small move toward what James labels here as "friendship with the world." Perhaps this true story will alert us to the hazard of small things.

When the massive Teton Dam in Southeastern Idaho collapsed on June 5, 1976, everyone was stunned. Without warning, under clear skies, the huge earthen structure suddenly gave way, sending millions of gallons of water surging into the Snake

River basin. A sudden catastrophe? An instantaneous disaster? It certainly seemed to be, from all outward appearances. But underneath, below the waterline where the engineers couldn't see, a hidden fault had been ever-so-gradually weakening the entire structure. It started small enough. Just a little weak spot, a little bit of erosion. No one saw it and it went untended. By the time the fault was detected, it was too late. The workmen on the dam barely had time to run for their lives and escape being swept away. No one saw the little flaw, but everyone saw the big collapse.[29]

As we examine James's teaching here on friendship with the world versus friendship with God, ask God to reveal any "small things" in your life that may be a signal of a budding friendship with the world!

James 4:4-6

[4] Adulterers and adulteresses! Do you not know that friendship with the world is enmity with God? Whoever therefore wants to be a friend of the world makes himself an enemy of God.

[5] Or do you think that the Scripture says in vain, "The Spirit who dwells in us yearns jealously"?

[6] But He gives more grace. Therefore He says: "God resists the proud, but gives grace to the humble."

God's Message...

1. We've seen James address his readers as "my brethren" and "my beloved brethren," but how does he address them here in verse 4?

And what question does he have for them (and us) in verse 4?

And what statement of fact does he make in verse 4?

2. When it comes to the proud, what action does God take against them (verse 6)?

And how does God assist the humble (verse 6)?

...and Your Heart's Response

- "Adulterers and adulteresses" is James's way of addressing (and with shock value!) those who are spiritually unfaithful to God, those who are making pleasure the chief end of life. Can you think of any areas where you may be flirting with worldliness and with the pleasures of this world? Or, can you think of areas of worldliness that tempt every Christian?

> *B*eware of such temptation and worldly pleasures! For…
>
> …[they are] like the ivy with the oak. The ivy may give the oak a grand, beautiful appearance, but all the while it is feeding on its vitals. Are we compromising with the enemies of God? Are we being embraced by the world, by its honors, its pleasures, its applause? This may add to us in the world's estimation, but our strength becomes lost.[30]

- There's no getting around it—friendship with the world is hostility toward God! It's a fact. What's the first reason James gives us as to why we cannot be a friend of the world (verse 4)?

Have you ever thought about this *either/or* choice that James is addressing—that you're choosing to be *either* a friend to the world *or* a friend to God? Or, that you're choosing to be *either* an enemy toward the world *or* an enemy toward God? Search your own heart and consider the kinds of choices you've made during the past hour…or week…or year. According to the pattern of your choices, are you building a friendship with God…or with the world?

Jot down ways to "correct your course" and steer your choices away from the world and toward the Lord.

And remember this thought: "To maintain friendship with the world is to be on good terms with persons and forces and things that are at least indifferent toward God if not openly hostile to him, and thus to be an enemy of God."[31]

- When it comes to verse 5, James seems to be saying that God yearns to see His Spirit, the Holy Spirit, evidenced in our lives. Those who are humbly seeking to live wholly for God will receive the gracious help needed from God to enable them to do just that. In other words, God blesses the humble-minded and favors the lowly with his continual grace.

At the same time, God is opposed to the proud and sets Himself against them. *Opposes* is a military word and means that God actually wages war against the proud and arrays Himself against the haughty.

Before we leave this lesson, see if you can think of three ways you can humbly seek a life that pleases God and enjoys the assistance of His great and marvelous grace.

From the Heart of a Woman

There is a chorus in a long-loved hymn, dear one, that shows us the way to a life of friendship with God. Hear its sweet words:

> Turn your eyes upon Jesus,
> Look full in His wonderful face,
> And the things of earth will grow strangely dim
> In the light of His glory and grace.[32]

When we turn our eyes upon Jesus, we won't be interested in the small trinkets that the world offers. When we turn our eyes upon Jesus, we'll be consumed with *Him*—the light of His glory and grace, instead of consumed with *them*—the pale things of this world. When we turn our eyes upon Jesus, the small things will cease to matter, for then we will be utterly absorbed in Him, our precious Savior.

Lesson 18

Drawing Near to God

*J*hope you have a sense of humor. And while I know there's nothing humorous regarding these verses from James about what it means to submit ourselves humbly to God, I did run across this funny incident that illustrates the message of this passage well.

It seems that a certain preacher wrote a letter to a sister church that was struggling with an internal dispute and at the same time wrote yet another letter to the manager of his farm. In error the letters went into the wrong envelopes. Therefore, when the minister's letter arrived at the ailing church, it read, "Keep down the weeds. Keep up the fences. And keep a sharp lookout for the old black bull."

The elder in charge solemnly read the wise counselor's advice and said, "My brethren, it is not difficult to interpret this parable. The weeds are causes of dissension, and we are advised therefore to see to it that no root of bitterness is allowed to grow up among us.

"The fences are undoubtedly intended to represent church discipline.

"Then, of course, my brethren, you will readily recognize who is meant by the big, black bull. That can be no other than the devil himself.

"What we are admonished to do, therefore, is to keep down all causes of possible dissension, maintain strict discipline, and always be on the alert to resist the approach of the devil. If we follow this advice, no doubt the garden of the Lord will prosper."[33]

Now let's see what James has to say!

James 4:7-10

[7] Therefore submit to God. Resist the devil and he will flee from you.

[8] Draw near to God and He will draw near to you. Cleanse your hands, you sinners; and purify your hearts, you double-minded.

[9] Lament and mourn and weep! Let your laughter be turned to mourning and your joy to gloom.

[10] Humble yourselves in the sight of the Lord, and He will lift you up.

God's Message...

James is on a roll! He's opened up a subject—the subject of worldliness (James 4:4-6)—and he's not about to let go of it until he gives his readers a solution. After nine references to his readers as "my brethren" or "my beloved brethren" how does he refer to them in James, chapter 4...

...verse 4—

...verse 8a—

...verse 8b—

And now let's look at James's solution to the problem of worldliness. He gives ten commands for drawing near to God and turning away from the world. Can you find them? Also complete those that call for extra information.

Command 1—Verse 7a

Command 2—Verse 7b

Command 3—Verse 8

Command 4—Verse 8

Command 5—Verse 8

Command 6—Verse 9

Command 7—Verse 9

Command 8—Verse 9

Command 9—Verse 9

Command 10—Verse 10

...and Your Heart's Response

- As you consider the many messages and teachings of these four verses, what do you learn about the devil (verse 7)?

  Look at these further descriptions of the devil. Jot down the information given.

  2 Corinthians 11:14—

  1 Peter 5:8—

  According to Ephesians 6:10-17 what is the process whereby we can resist the devil?

  Can you think of others?

  Use your answers to these questions to formulate a strategy for resisting the devil. Write it out here...and perhaps in your Bible!

- What do you learn about drawing near to God in Hebrews 7:19? (Just a note: This means that it's through the high priesthood of Jesus Christ that we can as Christians "draw near to God.")

  And what do you learn about drawing near to God in Psalm 24:3-4?

  And in Psalm 145:18?

- This is not the first time that James has made reference to the struggle we're involved in for wholehearted faith and devotion to God. What was his message to us in James 1:7-8?

Here again in James 4:8 the spotlight is on divided loyalties—between satisfying ourselves and pleasing God. Can you think of any struggle you're currently facing in this area of double-mindedness and double-heartedness? And can you think of specific ways that you can scour and scrub and "purify your heart" from all that is unclean and impure in the eyes of God?

From the Heart of a Woman

Weeds, fences, and the old black bull.

Dear friend, I know you want to be a woman after God's own heart. And that means that you desire to draw near to God, to humble yourself in His sight, and to keep yourself pure from sin and make God your #1 Priority.

So watch out for the weeds of sin—pride, doubt, bitterness, envy, anger, and halfheartedness.

Keep the fences strong and high—against worldliness, lust, passion, and ungodly desires.

And by all means, watch out for the old black bull, the devil himself—resist him firmly and take your stand against him.

Heeding James's "ten commandments" is how you and I can grow in wisdom and faith and give God first priority in our hearts. Won't you give Him your wholehearted, devoted allegiance?

Refusing to Judge Others

ecently I read this personal advice from Charles Swindoll that certainly fits this lesson as we consider one more time James's words to us on the subject of slander and judging others. Dr. Swindoll wrote, "Perhaps like me you've received a phone call from someone who says, 'I want to tell you about so-and-so.' And I'll say, 'Wait a minute. May I quote you?' There's usually a long pause. And then they'll say, 'Well, I'm not sure that would be a good idea.' Invariably my answer would be, 'Then I'm not interested in hearing what you have to say.'" Then he added, "Gossip and rumor have ruined many a soul, haven't they?"[34]

The answer is, of course, a resounding *yes!*

As we begin, please remember what has gone before. James has taught us that selfishness and a lack of humility lead to a worldly lifestyle (James 4:1-6). And here is yet more evidence of worldliness—speaking evil of others. Read on...and take note.

James 4:11-12

¹¹ Do not speak evil of one another, brethren. He who speaks evil of a brother and judges his brother, speaks evil of the law and judges the law. But if you judge the law, you are not a doer of the law but a judge.

¹² There is one Lawgiver, who is able to save and to destroy. Who are you to judge another?

God's Message...

1. In our last passage, we saw James give us ten commands for drawing near to God. What command does he give here (verse 11)?

Why does James say this is such a serious issue (verse 11)?

And if we do so, what happens (verse 11)?

2. And why does James say this is absurd (verse 12)?

What final question does James ask (verse 12)?

...and Your Heart's Response

- It helps us to realize that there's a natural (and sinful) progression that James is dealing with in these few verses, and that progression begins in the preceding verses. He's pointing out that selfishness and a failure to subject and humble ourselves before God leads us to speak evil of our brothers and sisters in Christ. James has already spent 18 verses (James 3:1-18) on the matter of the tongue...and now here it is again!

  Did you know that to speak evil of someone means to talk them down? It's a form of belittling as well as talking behind their back—i.e. backbiting. And James is concerned that believers in the body, brothers and sisters in Christ, would do this to one another. Let's look (again!) at a few other scriptures on this lethal subject. Take notes as you go.

  Romans 1:29-30—(these are marks of ungodly unbelievers)

  2 Corinthians 12:20—(these are the sins Paul feared he would find in the church at Corinth)

  Ephesians 4:31—(a command from Paul)
  And what is the solution (verse 32)?

  Colossians 3:8—(a command from Paul)
  And what is the solution (verses 12 and 14)?

  1 Peter 2:1—(this is Peter's formula for spiritual growth)

> *As* one wise teacher writes, "Not only is slander a devastating sin, it is also a [widespread] one. While other sins require a particular set of circumstances before they can be committed, slander needs only a malicious tongue driven by hatred."[35]

- James next moves to the law and explains that to judge a Christian is to set oneself up as a judge of God's moral law—the royal law of love which states that we should love one another. Then James gives a second reason for not speaking evil and judging one another—that to do so is to set oneself above God, who is the Lawgiver! In words put by another, "How ridiculous, how futile, for incompetent and ignorant man to take it upon himself to judge his brother. No wonder James asks, 'Who do you think you are?'"[36]

    Look at the following admonitions from God. What are we to do instead of "throwing down" the reputation and good name of another? Instead of maligning and backbiting, what does God desire from us?

Leviticus 19:18—

Mark 12:30-31—

James 2:8—

- When others do sin, what guidelines does the Bible give us in Matthew 18:15-17 for the proper handling of such a situation?

From the Heart of a Woman

Oh, dear friend! Are you beginning to sense the gravity of this whole area of gossip and slander? It hurts all parties—especially the one we malign—and it hurts the Lord's body of believers.

We have a choice to make about the kind of words we speak. We can speak...or not speak. We can destroy...or we can build. We can spread hatred...or love. We can discourage...or encourage. We can scream...or speak softly. We can cut...or comfort.

Why not whisper a prayer to the God who asks us "to speak evil of no one" (Titus 3:2)? Why not begin making (by God's grace!) the choice not to speak evil of one another? Why not refuse to judge others?

A careless word may kindle strife.

A cruel word may wreck a life.

A brutal word may smite and kill.

A gracious word may smooth the way.

A joyous word may light the day.

A timely word may lessen stress.

A loving word may heal and bless.

—Walter[37]

Lesson 20

Planning with Wisdom

James 4:13-17

Are you a planner, dear one? Do you have a life management system for planning and organizing your time so that you accomplish what you must...and maybe a little more? Most of the women I know have some sort of notebook set up to organize their tasks and roles and responsibilities as busy women with people to serve and work to accomplish.

I have such a planner (actually, more than one!) for my days, my family, my home, my projects, my relationships, and my ministries. Not only do I try to break my activities down into tasks, but I also have a plan for follow-up. Planning is a must for me!

Well, as we step into James's classroom once again, we find him lecturing today on time management and planning—*divine style!* He's showing us *God's way* to plan.

There's nothing wrong with planning and organization (indeed, the Bible has much to say about time and its careful oversight), but there are a few rules James says we must be sure to follow. So pay attention as James points us to two conditions we must never violate!

James 4:13-17

[13] Come now, you who say, "Today or tomorrow we will go to such and such a city, spend a year there, buy and sell, and make a profit";

[14] whereas you do not know what will happen tomorrow. For what is your life? It is even a vapor that appears for a little time and then vanishes away.

[15] Instead you ought to say, "If the Lord wills, we shall live and do this or that."

[16] But now you boast in your arrogance. All such boasting is evil.

[17] Therefore, to him who knows to do good and does not do it, to him it is sin.

God's Message...

1. As James addresses his Jewish readers who carried on a lucrative trade throughout the area of the Mediterranean Sea, he speaks to those who were known to make expansive plans for their business enterprises. What does James report that they were supposedly saying about their future (verse 13)?

What statement of fact does James make about those who make such declarations regarding the future (verse 14a)?

2. Next comes a question asked down through the ages. What is that question (verse 14)?

And how does James, under the inspiration of the Holy Spirit of God, answer this profound question (verse 14)?

3. Not content merely to confront his readers, James goes on to correct them. What better thing ought they to say instead when they make their plans (verse 15)?

4. Can you find the three negative words James employs to point out the seriousness of their presumptuous planning (verse 16)?

James follows up these three negatives with yet another stunning one—"sin"! What does he say is a sin (verse 17)?

...and Your Heart's Response

• Throughout James's letter to his believing Jewish readers, he's been hammering away at attitudes, actions, and words that run contrary to those that should mark out a pure faith. As he has said before, "These things ought not to be so" (James 3:10)! Here in chapter 4 he strikes at the attitude of arrogance and self-sufficiency in presuming on the future.

In Luke 12:16-21, note God's condemnation of the rich man and his self-sufficiency. What was the rich man thinking? And what was he planning? And what did God call this man?

Rather than leaving God out of our thoughts and plans, what does James say to do (or say) instead (verse 15)?

What good example does the apostle Paul set for us in planning?

Acts 18:21—

1 Corinthians 4:19—

1 Corinthians 16:7—

• We noted earlier that there are two conditions we should be careful not to violate in our decision-making and planning. The *first* is failing to consider our finiteness as human beings. Let's face it—our knowledge is limited! We have no way of knowing what the future holds for us. The *second* is failing to consider the uncertainty of life, which James describes as a vapor, or a puff of smoke. James's readers had a warped view of themselves *and* of life *and* of God. Theirs was a sin of omission—of omitting God as they planned!

   How are you when it comes to including God in your planning sessions? Do you pray over your plans? When you speak of the future—even the next hour—do you add to your thoughts and words, "Lord willing...if the Lord wills"? What specific practices will you follow to guard against leaving God out and to correct such "practical atheism"? After you answer this final question, read the exhortation below.

> *J*ames is not against making plans...he is not taking a cheap shot at charts or making an argument against commitments....What James warns us about is that our freedom to make plans is not a license to live free from God. To come to that conclusion would be arrogant....The phrase, "If it is the Lord's will" ought to infect our thinking. It ought to be a standard part of our vocabulary.[38]

- Arrogance. Boasting. Evil. Sin. Indeed, James holds nothing back when pointing his finger at our disobedience! Once again, what is his definition of sin in verse 17? (You may want to memorize it!)

James begins a summary here in verse 17 with the word "Therefore." He's definitely wrapping up his exhortation to his readers regarding their practice of planning without considering the Lord's will. But he's also wrapping up chapters 1-4. It's one thing not to know what the Bible teaches—what the will of the Lord is and what we're not to do. But it's another to know and to choose not to obey. And now that James has painstakingly labored for four chapters to address one area of conduct after another, his readers (and you and I, too) now know what is right and what is wrong.

What is the pattern of your life? Are you a "doer of the Word"? When you discover some new counsel from the Lord, do you leap immediately into action, ensuring that you "do" what you've learned and making your new knowledge about God's will become an embedded part of your life? Or do you wait, hanging on to a few favorite sins, before you (and *if* you) relinquish them and do the right thing, as James says? As writer Elisabeth Elliot has noted, "Delayed obedience is disobedience." It may help you to write out a prayer of personal commitment to a life of greater obedience.

From the Heart of a Woman

As a woman after God's own heart who desires to grow in wisdom and plan in wisdom, what are God's guidelines for goal-setting? Here are a few.

1. Realize only God knows your future.
2. Realize God has a purpose for your life.
3. Realize God may send interruptions into your perfect day.
4. Remember to pray over your plans. Ask God for His help and guidance as you plan your day...or your life.
5. Remember to say, "If the Lord wills...."

Lesson 21

Calculating the Truth About Wealth

As I was studying this next section of James's letter to the scattered Jewish believers of his day, I ran across several stories about the misuse of wealth and about the wrong attitudes we can have toward material goods. One is quite typical and the other is outright defiant! Let's allow these two stories to not only instruct us but to prepare our hearts for James's latest words of wisdom.

> *Story One*—A certain young person very impatiently said, "I'm living now, and I mean to have a good time. The hereafter isn't here yet!" A very wise companion replied, "No—only the first part of it; but I shouldn't wonder if the 'here' had a good deal to do with shaping the 'after.'"

Story Two—A farmer who prided himself to be an agnostic wrote a letter to a local newspaper, saying, "Sir, I have been trying an experiment with a field of mine. I plowed it on Sunday. I planted it on Sunday. I cultivated it on Sunday. I reaped it on Sunday. I hauled it into my barn on Sunday. And now, Mr. Editor, what is the result? I have more bushels to the acre in that field than any of my neighbors have had this October." The editor wasn't a religious man himself, but he published the letter and then wrote below it: "God does not always settle His accounts in October."[39]

James 5:1-6

¹ Come now, you rich, weep and howl for your miseries that are coming upon you!

² Your riches are corrupted, and your garments are moth-eaten.

³ Your gold and silver are corroded, and their corrosion will be a witness against you and will eat your flesh like fire. You have heaped up treasure in the last days.

⁴ Indeed the wages of the laborers who mowed your fields, which you kept back by fraud, cry out; and the cries of the reapers have reached the ears of the Lord of Sabaoth.

⁵ You have lived on the earth in pleasure and luxury; you have fattened your hearts as in a day of slaughter.

⁶ You have condemned, you have murdered the just; he does not resist you.

God's Message...

1. James here aims his message at a particular group. Who are they, and what does he tell them to do (verse 1)?

2. There were three obvious signs of wealth in the day in which James wrote—food (or, as James labels it, "riches"), clothing, and precious metals. What does James have to say about each?

   Food (verse 2)—

   Clothing (verse 2)—

   Precious metals (verse 3)—

   Notice that James does not address the wealthy in these verses as "brethren." Instead he informs them of impending judgment. When judgment comes, what role will their wealth play (verse 3)?

3. How does James say this particular group had obtained their riches (verse 4)?

   He also mentions two "voices." List them here (verse 4).

   And how far had their cry gone (verse 4)?

4. Next follows four indictments against the rich. List them here (verses 5-6).

And how had the poor responded (verse 6)?

...and Your Heart's Response

* Is it wrong to have wealth? James does not address that issue. He instead is pointing to the *means* by which wealth is amassed. In the case cited here in James 5, riches came at the expense of others. Jot down what God says about the dangers of money.

  Proverbs 22:16—

  Matthew 6:24—

  Luke 18:24—

  1 Timothy 6:10—

* What advice does God give about money?

  Romans 13:6-7—

  Romans 13:8—

  1 Corinthians 16:2—

  2 Corinthians 9:7—

  1 Timothy 5:8—

  1 Timothy 6:17-18—

From the Heart of a Woman

Economists tell us that we're living in a golden age. Unemployment is down. Income is up. And spending is up. Yet, the Bible makes it clear that the "good times" will not last... and neither will our riches (James 1:10-11)! As I was thinking through this whole issue of money and wealth and riches, it seems that James is calling us to a better *attitude* toward money. We must remember that everything (including wealth) comes from God. We must also remember that eternal life is much more important than temporal wealth—and that money can't buy salvation! We must remember, too, (as James has already instructed us—see James 2:1-9) not to show favoritism to the rich. And, as Paul advised, we must remember to be content...in whatever condition we find ourselves, whether in plenty or in want (Philippians 4:10-12).

But, dear woman of faith, we must go into *action* when it comes to extending God's mercy to the poor and needy, regardless of what we do or don't have. Here are a few first steps in giving:

1. Begin at home—by providing the basics for those under your own roof.
2. Give regularly to your home church—which in turn gives to those in need.
3. Keep your ear to the ground—and take note of those who are struggling. Ignorance is *not* bliss when it comes to people in need!
4. Support a worthy organization or person.
5. Err on the side of generosity.
6. Live out love—regardless of your finances, you have much to give and can bless many by giving God's love.[40]

Lesson 22

Putting On a Heart of Patience

*I*know there are a lot of jokes made about patience ("Patience is the ability to count to ten before blasting off!" "Lord, I need patience, and I need it *now!*"), but when you're the one who's forced to wait while you suffer—or suffer while you wait—it's no laughing matter!

Ponder instead this thought-provoking description of the pain and purpose of waiting as given in the introduction of author and pastor Ben Patterson's book, *Waiting*. He writes, "Picture a blazing hot forge and a piece of gold thrust into it to be heated until all that is impure and false is burnt out. As it is heated, it is also softened and shaped by the metalworker. Our faith is the gold; our suffering is the fire. The forge is the waiting: it is the tension and longing and, at times, anguish of waiting for God to keep his promises."[41]

Dear one, in this lesson James speaks to us on the necessity of waiting patiently on the Lord. We know that David, too, encourages us to "Wait on the Lord; be of good courage, and He shall strengthen your heart; wait, I say, on the Lord!" (Psalm 27:14). I think you'll be glad to see how very practical James's advice is on this sorely-needed virtue of patience and how it is nurtured.

James 5:7-11

⁷ Therefore be patient, brethren, until the coming of the Lord. See how the farmer waits for the precious fruit of the earth, waiting patiently for it until it receives the early and latter rain.

⁸ You also be patient. Establish your hearts, for the coming of the Lord is at hand.

⁹ Do not grumble against one another, brethren, lest you be condemned. Behold, the Judge is standing at the door!

¹⁰ My brethren, take the prophets, who spoke in the name of the Lord, as an example of suffering and patience.

¹¹ Indeed we count them blessed who endure. You have heard of the perseverance of Job and seen the end intended by the Lord—that the Lord is very compassionate and merciful.

God's Message...

1. Read again James 5:6. It is to these "righteous" men who do not even resist ill treatment that James writes verses

7-11. How many times in this passage does James tell these suffering Christians to be patient?

And how long were they to be patient (verse 7)?

Ever the teacher, what illustration does James use to explain the process of waiting patiently (verse 7)?

And how long was the waiting process for those in James's example (verse 7)?

What other practical advice does James give for endurance under duress (verse 8)?

2. Suffering tends to cause us to lash out at others, at those closest to us. Therefore, what exhortation does James give for interpersonal relationships while suffering (verse 9)?

3. James next gives his readers two examples of patient suffering that they would be well acquainted with. Who are they (verses 10-11)?

Example #1—

Example #2—

Ending his plea for patience on a high note, what does James say about the character of God (verse 11)?

...and Your Heart's Response

- *Regarding the farmer*—The illustration of a farmer would have been very familiar to James's readers. A farmer plants his crops and then begins waiting for "the precious fruit of the earth" (verse 7). The farmer planted…but the produce lay in the providence of God: Rain was needed! Therefore, the farmer waited…patiently…for the early rains of the fall and for the late rains of spring.

  So we, too, when we suffer, are to wait patiently until the coming of the Lord. How are you when it comes to waiting? If "0" equals no patience at all, and "5" equals very patient, where would you rate yourself? Or, how do you think those who know you best would rate you?

  Is there something God is asking you to be patient about right now? List three immediate steps you will take to "be patient" while you wait on God to act.

- *Regarding the Lord*—Five times James mentions the Lord. What do you learn about Him in…

  Verse 7—

  Verse 8—

  Verse 9—

  Verse 10—

  Verse 11—

We wait for the coming of the Lord, just as the Greeks waited for the official visit of a monarch to their city. And the hope we derive from the promise of His coming helps us to wait patiently. When *He* arrives, *He* will set everything in order. *He* will make things right. He will correct all abuses. *He* will bring deliverance from all our suffering.

How does the fact of the second coming of the Lord encourage your heart as you endure through hard times?

Take a few notes on the following Scriptures. Then pick one of these sure words of faith and hope, circle it, memorize it, take it to heart...and look up!

Psalm 37:6-7—

Psalm 57:2—

Psalm 60:12—

Psalm 121:1-2—

Psalm 124:8—

Psalm 138:8—

- *Regarding the prophets and Job*—James points to the Old Testament prophets and to Job as examples of those who endured unjust suffering and trials. To familiarize yourself with the demise of the prophets, jot down a few notes as you look at...

  Nehemiah 9:26—

  Daniel 9:6—

  Matthew 23:31, 34-36—

  Acts 7:52—

To familiarize yourself with the story of Job, take notes on his sufferings and losses.

Job 1:14-19 (list Job's losses)—

Job 2:7—

What did James report that Job learned about God through his ordeal (James 5:11)?

To familiarize yourself with God's blessings on Job, read Job 42:12-17.

Write a few sentences about how these illustrations from the lives of the prophets and of Job strengthen your faith and your patience as you wait on the Lord.

From the Heart of a Woman

A woman who is growing in faith sets her hopes on the promises of God, and the promise of Jesus' arrival is the promise of what is to come. Where is your gaze fixed, dear sister? Downward...on the entangling evils, on the suffering you must endure, or upward...from whence He will come? (Or...are you one who thinks little about His coming?) Our patience is helped along as you and I look to the promise of His return. We live with "what is," but we have the promise of "what is to be." And in between we have our "waiting" time. We can either fret, worry, and pace, or we can put on a heart of patience (Colossians 3:12). Which will it be for you, dear one? Oh, I pray that you will choose to "be still [to be patient], and know that I am God [the Lord who is coming again and the Judge who is indeed standing at the door]" (Psalm 46:10)!

Praying Always

James 5:12-18

*J*ames has just about brought us full circle. In the first chapter of his epistle, verse 5, he wrote that we should pray and ask God for the wisdom we need to grow in the practicalities of true faith. And now he writes again in his closing words about prayer—about *effective, fervent* prayer! As one has commented, "If we can say that James's letter summarizes the work of faith, his conclusion focuses on faith's finest work—believers effective in prayer."[42]

Ever the to-the-point teacher, James instructs his readers (and us!) with a series of commands and an example of effective, fervent prayer. I know that as a woman after God's own heart you desire to make prayer a vital part of your daily life. So do I! So let's sit at James's feet for a most important message on the power of righteous praying.

James 5:12-18

¹² But above all, my brethren, do not swear, either by heaven or by earth or with any other oath. But let your "Yes" be "Yes," and your "No," "No," lest you fall into judgment.

¹³ Is anyone among you suffering? Let him pray. Is anyone cheerful? Let him sing psalms.

¹⁴ Is anyone among you sick? Let him call for the elders of the church, and let them pray over him, anointing him with oil in the name of the Lord.

¹⁵ And the prayer of faith will save the sick, and the Lord will raise him up. And if he has committed sins, he will be forgiven.

¹⁶ Confess your trespasses to one another, and pray for one another, that you may be healed. The effective, fervent prayer of a righteous man avails much.

¹⁷ Elijah was a man with a nature like ours, and he prayed earnestly that it would not rain; and it did not rain on the land for three years and six months.

¹⁸ And he prayed again, and the heaven gave rain, and the earth produced its fruit.

God's Message...

1. Before we approach James's words to us about being faithful in prayer, what command does he first give in verse 12?

And how does he preface his command?

What does James advise his readers to do instead of swearing?

2. As we noted above, James teaches by using a series of commands. Let's consider them one at a time. Find and write out each one of them.

- What is the suffering person to do (verse 13)?

- And the cheerful person (verse 13)?

- How about the one who is sick (verse 14)?

- And what are the elders of the church to do (verse 14)?

What does James say will happen as a result of prayer (verse 15)?

List the two "one anothers" James commands in verse 16.

Why does James say this is important (verse 16b)?

And what Old Testament example does James use in verses 17-18?

Quickly note the details surrounding this particular instance of prayer. (You may also enjoy reading the full story in 1 Kings 18:1,41-45.)

...and Your Heart's Response

James makes it very clear what we're to do about "swearing", about taking oaths. We're simply to use honest speech and say what we mean and mean what we say. With his point made, James then moves on to the subject of prayer. Oh, what we can learn in these few verses as James calls everyone in the entire church to prayer!

- *Those who are suffering*—This has specific reference to those who are being persecuted, abused, and mis-treated.[43] According to 1 Peter 5:6-7, how does prayer help those who suffer in this way?

- *Those who are cheerful*—Those who were fortunate enough to manage a cheerful attitude were to sing praises, another form of prayer. What do you learn about praise here?

    Ephesians 5:19—

    Colossians 3:16—

Summed up, James writes, in effect, "If you have a problem in your life because of circumstantial suffering, look to God in prayer. If everything is going well and you are cheerful, look to God with praise."[44]

Where does your life find you today, dear one? Are you suffering...or are you cheerful? Whichever it is, are you following James's instruction? What can you do to follow through more faithfully?

- *Those who are sick*—This verse indicates that...

  ...the *sick* one is to take action and call for the leaders or "elders" of the church,

  ...the *leaders* are to pray for the one who is ill, and

  ...the *faith-filled prayers* of the elders will restore those who are weak (physically and spiritually) and defeated to spiritual wholeness.

- *Those who have sinned*—James has a "bigger picture"[45] in mind, and that bigger picture is sin. His focus is not so much on oil and healing as it is on prayer and sin. Sin left unchecked can lead to God's chastisement in the form of severe and incapacitating illness. When this is the case, the sick one is to call for the elders and have them pray (verse 15).

  But James's general application (verse 16) is that *all* believers be sure to confess their sins and pray for each other. Do you have other Christians to whom you are accountable, my friend? With whom you may share and confide in regarding areas of sinfulness in your life? Others who will pray for you?

- *Those who pray*—We are all to confess our sin to others so that they may pray for us. But we are also all to be those who care, who listen, and who pray for others. Are you yourself one whom others can come to for faithful prayer on their behalf? Do you maintain a fervent prayer life?

From the Heart of a Woman

James, dear one, is just like a doctor who always knows what's best—even though it hurts! When we have a physical ailment, sometimes the treatment is painful. Surgery sets us back. Chemotherapy and radiation knock us down. Even stitches or injections hurt. Yet, in the end (Lord willing!) we're helped and relieved. Progress is made.

That's what James (and the Lord) wants for you and me—to be rid of any and every sin that harms us. And his treatment hurts! It's difficult to admit mistakes, to ask for prayer, and to seek forgiveness. But in the end we are better! And, as James points out, we avoid more severe chastisement.This poetry drawn from Psalm 32 shows us the weight of sin and the marvelous benefits of confessing our faults:

> While I kept guilty silence,
> my strength was spent with grief,
> Thy hand was heavy on me, my soul found no relief;
> But when I owned my trespass, my sin hid not from Thee
> When I confessed transgression, then Thou forgavest me.
> —Psalter[46]

So, don't you think it's awfully obvious what God is calling us to as women of true faith? We must seek to walk uprightly, admit our sin when we fail and fall, and appeal to others for their effectual prayers on our behalf, and do the same for others—praying always.

Demonstrating a Heart of Love

We're here! We've done it! We've made it through James's powerful epistle on becoming a dynamic believer who wisely lives out a faith that is true. I hope you've grown in wisdom and faith. I know it's been a wonderful (and sometimes jarring!) journey for me.

As we end James's letter today, we can't help but notice that he ends it rather abruptly. Unlike Paul, Peter, John, and Jude, there are no sweet parting words, no final blessing or benediction.

But James's closing is true to the tone of his entire letter. In no-nonsense, direct-and-to-the-point words, James delivers his final great challenge to all Christians, ending his epistle as an encouraging, supportive pastor.

Remember that James's letter has been brimming with do's and don'ts, but here he crowns his epistle with a powerful "do" when it comes to living out true faith. Let's see what it is...

James 5:19-20

¹⁹ Brethren, if anyone among you wanders from the truth, and someone turns him back,

²⁰ let him know that he who turns a sinner from the error of his way will save a soul from death and cover a multitude of sins.

God's Message...

Just to review from our previous lesson covering James 5:12-18, we considered a variety of people in a church body:

- those who swear (verse 12)
- those who are suffering (verse 13)
- those who are cheerful (verse 13)
- those who are sick (verses 14-15)
- those who have sinned (verse 16)
- those who pray (verses 16-18)

Now James adds one final category:

- those who wander from the truth.

Unfortunately there are people in every congregation who wander and stray from the truth, who profess salvation but fail to live it out.

1. What does James tell those in the church to attempt to do for the one who wanders from the truth (verse 19)?

2. And what does James say the twofold results of restoring such a one will be (verse 20)?

   a.

   b.

...and Your Heart's Response

- *Others*—Jot down several not-so-godly responses church members may sometimes have toward those who stray from the truth.

  After considering James's instruction, what will you seek to do for the wandering soul?

  Paul has advice for us, too, about how to assist those who have erred. Look at Galatians 6:1-2 and take notes.

  Matthew, too, has advice for us. Look at Matthew 18:12-14 and take notes.

  Do you know anyone you need to talk to today who is straying from the truth?

- *Ourselves*—It's one thing to watch out for others, but a woman of true faith must also watch out for herself! Have you heard the saying that goes something like this—"You are either moving forward or backward—there is no such thing as standing still in the Christian life"? As one gentleman, who uses the term "backsliding" to describe the wandering and erring soul, notes, "Do you know what you have to do to backslide? Nothing!"[47] In other words, our passivity and the doing of "nothing" can have a disastrous effect on our spiritual growth.

Take a moment to look at 2 Peter 1:5-10. What are some practical things Peter says you and I can do to further grow in our faith?

Jot down any steps you need to take today...this week...this month to promote forward movement.

There's another way that we wander from the truth and that's by actively turning away from what is best to what is second-best. Are there any "second-best" choices you're currently making or have made in the past that are actively leading you away from your "first love" (Revelation 2:4)? How do you plan to set your feet once again on the highway of the righteous (Proverbs 16:17)?

From the Heart of a Woman

"The end." That's it. James is over. And exactly what is it that James wants for us as women of true faith and wisdom? He wants us to be sure that we are about the business of going after those who are straying from the truth. And when we do so, the blessings are threefold:

We assist a sinner to turn from the error of his ways,

We assist God in saving a soul from death, and

We help to cover a multitude of sins.

I've given much thought to these final two verses. And, as I went through the next exercise and re-read the book of James, noting all of the behaviors James condemns (like partiality and judging, unbridled speech against others, strife and bickering), I noticed that he chooses to end with the better "works" of love. James calls us away from the negative works that have no place in a Christian or in a group of believers in Christ...and calls us instead to pray for one another (James 5:16) and to love enough and to care enough to pursue (rather than judge and gossip about) those who are wandering. This kind of love, dear one, helps convert the sinner from the error of his way and saves his soul from death!

So...which will it be? The works of love...or the works of loathing? The words of blessing...or the words of cursing. The pursuit of the sinner...or the passing of judgment?

Oh, dear woman of faith! May the *works* of your faith match the *words* of your faith! May the *practice* of your faith parallel the *profession* of your faith! May your *walk* align with your *talk!* For, as commentator Matthew Henry so eloquently observes,

> *T*hose that turn many to righteousness, and those who help to do so, shall shine as the stars for ever and ever.[48]

Lesson 25

Growing in Wisdom and Faith

Summary of James

As we leave the book of James and continue to live out his principles for growing in wisdom and faith, let's scan each chapter of James's letter. Record some thoughts in these spaces regarding the subject matter of each individual chapter. And please note—the first letter of each chapter title spells out the word **W-O-R-K-S**, pointing to the works of faith, true faith, which is the theme of James's epistle.[49]

Chapter 1: **W**-orking patience through trials

Some general thoughts about chapter 1:

- James makes it clear that God permits temptation but never sends it. There is no sin in being tempted.... Sin comes when we yield to temptation.

- James exhorts us to have a quick ear, cautious tongue, calm temper and a pure heart. Our words and works must be in harmony.

- James does not teach that *works* form the *way* of salvation, but are simply the evidence of it. We do not work to be saved; we work because we are saved.[50]

Look into the mirror (so to speak) mentioned in James 1:23-25. Are you meeting your trials head-on with joy? Are your words and works in harmony? Are you a doer of the word and not merely a hearer? Do your "works" manifest a true faith?

Chapter 2: **O**-bedience that accompanies faith

Some general thoughts about chapter 2:

- James makes it clear that saintliness and snobbishness cannot exist together. Favoritism in churches is abominable. Riches must never come before religion, clothes before character, and position before piety. The poor must never be despised.

- Works cannot save, but they are evidence of our salvation.

- Abraham and Rahab are quoted as illustrations of faith.[51]

Are you a friend to the poor? How does your faith match up with that of Abraham and Rahab? Are there enough works of saving faith, enough "evidence," to "convict" you of being a Christian?

Chapter 3: **R**-estraining the unbridled tongue

Some general thoughts about chapter 3:

- Here James discourses on the sins of speech. How innumerable are the sins of uncontrolled tongues!

- There are sins of speech about ourselves—our tongues boast great things.

- There are sins of speech about others—our tongues utter harsh words or flatter unduly.

- There are sins of speech in connection with Christ's cause—our tongues disparage other workers, criticize when they should be silent.[52]

Do you pray about your speech? Is your speech seasoned with grace (Colossians 4:6)?

Chapter 4: **K**-eeping calm in conflicts

Some general thoughts about chapter 4:

- Seeking the friendship of the world, we become unfaithful to our divine Lover.

- Christ and the world are opposites, and the saint cannot have both. It is not Christ *and* the world, but Christ *or* the world.[53]

Are you one who seeks the will of the Lord in *all* things? Or are you one who merely talks much about the will of God?

Chapter 5: **S**-uffering and sick saints

Some general thoughts about chapter 5:

- James has some wise things to say about the grace of patience. When persecuted by the ungodly, or up against the collision of feeling among ourselves, we have need of patience.

- Encouragements to patience are before us in Christ's return, as well as in the example of the saints of old.

- The apostle tells us how to meet various experiences, such as depression and sickness. Songs should be mingled with our sobs.

- What a great passage on intercession is found here!

- The last word of James deals with soul-winning.[54]

Does looking to Christ's return help you with patience in the face of suffering? Are you in the habit of mingling songs with your sobs? Are you going about the business of seeing that sinners are converted?

Notes

1. Taken from Elizabeth George, *A Woman After God's Own Heart*™ (Eugene, OR: Harvest House Publishers, 1997) pp. 24-29.

2. *Life Application Bible Commentary —James* (Wheaton, IL: Tyndale House Publishers, Inc., 1992), p. 2.

3. Drawn from William Barclay, *The Letters of James and Peter,* rev. ed. (Philadelphia: The Westminster Press, 1976), pp. 35-36.

4. Harold D. Foos, *Faith in Practice* (Chicago: The Moody Bible Institute, 1984), pp. 34-35.

5. Herbert Lockyer, Sr., *A Devotional Commentary—Psalms* (Grand Rapids, MI: Kregel Publications, 1993), pp. 63-64.

6. Source unknown.

7. George, *A Woman After God's Own Heart*™, p. 29, quoting Jim Downing, *Meditation, The Bible Tells You How* (Colorado Springs: NavPress, 1976), pp. 15-16.

8. *Life Application Bible Commentary—James,* pp. 22-23.

9. Charles Spurgeon, *The Quotable Spurgeon* (Wheaton, IL: Harold Shaw Publishers, 1990), p. 292.

10. Edith Doan, *The Speaker's Sourcebook,* quoting Wallace Boys (Grand Rapids, MI: Zondervan Publishing House, 1977), p. 113.

11. Adapted and abridged from H. D. M. Spence and Joseph S. Exell, *The Pulpit Commentary, Volume 21—James* (Grand Rapids, MI: William B. Eerdmans Publishing Company, 1978), pp. 14-15.

12. *Life Application Bible Commentary—James,* p. 30.

13. John MacArthur, Jr., *The MacArthur New Testament Commentary— James* (Chicago: Moody Press, 1998), p. 72.

14. M.R. DeHaan and Henry G. Bosch, *Our Daily Bread* (Grand Rapids, MI: Zondervan Publishing House, 1982), July 29.

15. MacArthur, *The MacArthur New Testament Commentary—James,* p. 88.

16. *Life Application Bible* (Wheaton, IL: Tyndale House Publishers, Inc., 1988), p. 1919.

17. MacArthur, *The MacArthur New Testament Commentary—James,* p. 93.

18. *Life Application Bible Commentary—James,* p. 45.

19. D.L. Moody, *Notes from My Bible and Thoughts from My Library* (Grand Rapids, MI: Baker Book House, 1979), p. 182.

20. Barclay, *The Letters of James and Peter,* p. 66.

21. Charles F. Pfeiffer and Everett F. Harrison, *The Wycliffe Bible Commentary* (Chicago: Moody Press, 1973), p. 1434.

22. DeHaan and Bosch, *Our Daily Bread,* April 26.

23. Barclay, *The Letters of James and Peter,* p. 81.

24. Gene A. Getz, *The Measure of a Woman* (Glendale, CA: Regal Books, A Division of G/L Publications, 1977), p. 32.

25. *Life Application Bible,* p. 1921.

26. Spurgeon, *The Quotable Spurgeon,* p. 336.

27. Moody, *Notes from My Bible and Thoughts from My Library,* quoting Aiken, pp. 356-57.

28. *Life Application Bible Commentary—James,* p. 92.

29. Luis Palau, *Heart After God* (Portland, OR: Multnomah Press, 1978), p. 68.

30. Moody, *Notes from My Bible and Thoughts from My Library,* quoting Denham Smith, p. 357.

31. Pfeiffer and Harrison, *The Wycliffe Bible Commentary,* quoting Ropes, p. 1437.

32. Helen H. Lemmel, "Turn Your Eyes upon Jesus."

33. A. Naismith, *A Treasure of Notes, Quotes, and Anecdotes,* quoting Dr. Herbert Lockyer (Grand Rapids, MI: Baker Book House, 1975), p. 250.

34. Charles R. Swindoll, *The Tale of the Tardy Oxcart* (Nashville, TN: Word Publishing, 1998), p. 575.

35. MacArthur, *The MacArthur New Testament Commentary—James,* p. 218.

36. Foos, *Faith in Practice,* p. 132.

37. Doan, *The Speaker's Sourcebook,* p. 287.

38. *The Leadership Bible,* quoting Haddon Robinson, *Decision Making by the Book* (Grand Rapids, MI: Zondervan Publishing House, 1998), p. 251.

39. J. Vernon McGee, *Thru the Bible with J. Vernon McGee,* Volume 5 (Pasadena, CA: Thru The Bible Radio, 1983), p. 666.

40. Drawn from Elizabeth George, *Beautiful in God's Eyes* (Eugene, OR: Harvest House Publishers, 1998), pp. 137-140.

41. Ben Patterson, *Waiting* (Downers Grove, IL: InterVarsity Press, 1989), p. 11.

42. *Life Application Bible Commentary—James,* p. 137.

43. MacArthur, *The MacArthur New Testament Commentary—James,* p. 275.

44. Richard Mayhue, *The Healing Promise* (Eugene, OR: Harvest House Publishers, 1994), p. 130.

45. Ibid., pp. 135-36.

46. Richard W. DeHaan and H. G. Bosch, *Our Daily Bread Favorites* (Grand Rapids, MI: Zondervan Publishing House, 1971), June 12.

47. Albert M. Wells, Jr., *Inspiring Quotations—Contemporary & Classical,* quoting J. Donald Freese (Nashville: Thomas Nelson Publishers, 1988), p. 12.

48. Matthew Henry, *Commentary on the Whole Bible* (Peabody, MA: Hendricksen Publishers, 1996), p. 806.

49. Acrostic from Barry Huddleston, *The Acrostic Bible* (Portland, OR: Walk Thru the Bible Press, Inc., 1978).

50. Herbert Lockyer, *All the Books and Chapters of the Bible* (Grand Rapids, MI: Zondervan Publishing House, 1978), pp. 280-82.

51. Ibid.

52. Ibid.

53. Ibid.

54. Ibid.